Latin American Leaders

Latin American Leaders

BY

HAROLD E. DAVIS

Professor of History
The American University
Washington, D. C.

THE H. W. WILSON COMPANY
New York   1949

To
Barbara Lee

ACKNOWLEDGMENTS

Numerous persons have made valuable suggestions during the progress of this work. Those of Professor A. Curtis Wilgus of George Washington University, and Dr. Samuel Guy Inman, of New York, have been particularly helpful. The author is greatly indebted to Professor John E. Englekirk, of Tulane University, for reading the sketch on Rubén Darío, and to Dr. Paul Radin, of Berkeley, California, for criticizing the one on Fernández de Lizardi. Needless to say, their assistance does not in anyway relieve the author of full responsibility for all statements made. The staffs of the Cleveland Public Library, of the Hispanic Foundation and, especially, of the Columbus Memorial Library of the Pan American Union have given much valuable bibliographical assistance, which is gratefully acknowledged. The sketches on Irigoyen and Ingenieros were published in *World Affairs*, with the understanding on the part of The American Peace Society that they would also appear in this volume.

H.E.D.

CONTENTS

INTRODUCTION

POLITICAL THOUGHT AND LEADERSHIP IN LATIN AMERICA

Behind every great historical movement stand great men. To say this is not to endorse the fallacy that great men, through sheer exercise of will, or through some mystic link with deity or with destiny *make* history. So naive a concept will find few serious advocates today. Nor is leadership an automatic product of the working of social forces, in the sense that the situation always produces the man. If that were true the history of human civilization would not be, as it has been, full of great frustrations, tragedies, the decline of great cultures, the breakup of societies. Indeed, man lives constantly under the threat of the collapse of his civilization, erected at such great pains over the centuries, and only a series of miracles keeps this civilization alive. At the heart of such miracles a great leader will frequently be found.

Nor is mankind in the large entirely passive itself in this process, mechanically obeying certain social "laws." At times it shows greater and at times less dynamic force than circumstances would lead the investigator to expect. Hence it is, that in the study of historical developments, a little area of mystery frequently remains to defy the curiosity of the student who attempts to determine why a certain people is capable of great action at one moment in history, less capable at another. It is at this point that leadership plays an important part. The man who senses the meaning of his times is the extraordinary man in any age, and he may exercise great influence. This influence derives not so much from him, probably, as from the currents of social change which he represents and expresses. When, however, by a fortunate juncture of circumstances, such a person is placed in a position to have a decisive voice in the turn of events, and displays in his personality the qualities of winning confidence, commanding respect, and even compelling the action of others by the force of his will—then his leadership may have profound effect. Call him the instrument of history if you will, but he is an active, not a passive instrument. Say his power is not in himself but in those who accept his leadership. All this is true, but in spite of all this, the leader is in a real sense a man of judgment and intelligence, exercising real freedom of choice and will in accordance with these unusual gifts and attainments.

This volume continues the studies of Latin American leaders begun in a previous volume, *Makers of Democracy in Latin America*. It was not to be expected that the selection of twenty-four personages for brief study in that book, chiefly with a view to making their achievements better known to intelligent North Americans, would fail to encounter some criticism. Probably no one could select a list of twenty-four which would satisfy all readers. Many important historical figures were omitted, some of them unquestionably more important that some of those included. Although the list grows longer with the sixteen personages added in this volume there are many others, of course, who might be added. The biographical sketches in this book are somewhat fuller than those of the preceding volume. Many of the former were written for *The Cleveland Plain Dealer,* and within the strict space limitations of a newspaper column. No such limitation has affected those of the present volume, although the author has tried to confine himself to reasonably brief sketches.

Not all the leaders treated in the *Makers of Democracy in Latin America* were radical democrats. Several, such as Diego Portales of Chile, Bernardo Pereira de Vasconcellos of Brazil and Juan B. Alberdi of Argentina were definitely conservatives. Several readers, indeed, have questioned the propriety of including Portales, the strong man of Chile, and the conservative imperialist statesman, Vasconcellos, in any book on democracy. They may also question the inclusion of persons like Andrés Bello and the Imperial Regent, Feijó, in the present work.

In this connection it seems important, therefore, to state clearly the author's point of view on this fundamental question. It is his firm conviction that no study of democratic leadership is complete which fails to include generous representation of conservative leadership. In Latin America, as in the United States, democracy has required and profited from both conservative and liberal-progressive or radical leadership, in action and in ideas. In many cases it has been the conservative leaders rather than the radicals who have given the most constructive guidance in framing constitutions and in establishing the institutions essential to democratic life. The radical agitators are an important, an essential component of democratic life. Some of them, but not all, prove to be capable administrators. Many of them, in fact, have become dictators, while conservatives have often proved to be better democrats, or at least more constructive political leaders, in the final analysis.

It was a rather conservative group of landowners of São Paulo, led by José Bonifacio de Andrada and his brothers, who took the initiative in the movement for Brazilian independence. They believed themselves to be liberals, but when faced with the excesses of some of the new "exalted" liberals, turned conservative. Similarly, conservative forces played an important role in the mid-nineteenth century in shaping the constitution of the limited monarchy. Vasconcellos, whose career under the Brazilian Empire suggests in some respects that of the North American, John C. Calhoun, joined in the movement which forced the abdication of Pedro I, and was the author of the *Ato Adicional* of 1834 which established provincial autonomy and made the imperial ministers responsible to the Congress. But, like Calhoun, he was irrevocably attached to the interests of the conservative landowners which he represented, and so was drawn to the defense of slavery and into opposition to further reform. He was one of the great advocates of order and stability, adopting a typically conservative position. Yet, throughout, he and many of his party [1] were firm advocates of the principle of rule by the majority party in Congress, and of its supremacy over the ministers. They thus contributed immeasurably to laying the basis for the Brazilian republic.

Many other examples might be cited from other countries to show the essential role of conservative leaders in a democracy. In many cases, to be sure, it is difficult to draw closely the line which separates leadership of this kind from that which aims simply at personal power or even at reaction which seeks to destroy democracy. Augustín Iturbide of Mexico is a tantalizing figure from this standpoint—one which the author has not ventured to include in the present work because of the highly charged air of controversy which still characterizes the historical treatments of his political career. Doubtless some of the figures included in this volume may bring the same criticism—that they are leaders whose political role is still a matter of controversy—in spite of the author's effort to deal only with those leaders about whom it is possible to write with some assurance.

A difficult problem, and one which, in the author's judgment, has received all too little serious attention from students of Latin American history, is the problem of satisfactory classifications and satisfactory terminology for the various types of political leadership which have appeared in the history of that area. North Americans still tend too much to dismiss them all as dictators or constitutional executives, militarists or civilians, *caudillos* or non-*caudillos*. This is too easy and too simple, and presents, moreover a number of semantic difficulties. For there is, if anything, less agreement on the exact meaning of these terms than upon their use. Not that these classifications can be dispensed with, or that they are necessarily invalid. To a certain extent they are inevitable and, given some measure of agreement as to their meaning in use, they may be very useful in helping to understand the nature of political life at a given moment in a nation's history. But all such classifications have little meaning except in relation to a certain set of circumstances and conditions, and these vary so widely from time to time as to make such simple classifications largely meaningless. The dictatorships of Bernardo O'Higgins in Chile, of Mariano Melgarejo in Bolivia, of Juan Rosas in Argentina, of Juan Vicente Gómez in Venezuela,

---

[1] Originally a moderate, during the 1830's Vasconcellos became a member of the party of *regresso* which opposed Feijó and the moderates, and eventually joined forces with the conservatives who had supported Pedro I and worked for his return to Brazil. The *regresso* party opposed the move of the liberals to declare Pedro II of age.

of Santa Ana in Mexico, and of Getulio Vargas in Brazil have something in common, to be sure—the principle of arbitrary rule. But the character and tendencies, and the social import of their rule vary as widely from one case to the other as do the forces and circumstances responsible for the existence of the various regimes.

The types of political leadership are not few, but many, and the lines of demarcation between them are frequently not clear or precise. Yet certain types can be distinguished. If one approaches the problem by asking first, the objectives and policies which certain leaders have pursued and, second, the forces and circumstances which produced them, certain types begin to appear at once. Viewing the procession of Latin American political leaders from the standpoint of policies and objectives, one readily distinguishes opportunistic adventurers, radical reformers, overly optimistic visionaries, realists of conservative tendencies and realistic conservatives of a progressive or reforming bent, outright reactionaries, representatives of special interests, especially of class interests, nationalists, internationalists, and so on. Considering them from the standpoint of the forces and circumstances from which they sprang, one sees representatives of cities and urban interests on one hand, and on the other, rough leaders produced in the isolation of the sparsely inhabited, isolated provinces, inspired by provincial resentment and jealousy. One sees, also, leaders who have arisen from among the masses of underprivileged Indians and Negroes, or from the mixed racial groups so prominent in many Latin American countries. Sometimes they represent their groups of origin, and sometimes not. There are representatives of the army, of the church, of various important economic interests, such as mining, the cattle industry, or sugar production; strong men who arose in times of anarchy; leaders who were produced or sustained in periods of prosperity by new sources of national wealth; and men who represent various combinations of these factors.

But while most of these leaders are in some respect representatives of social classes or groups or of certain recognizable economic interests, it would be a mistake to assume that these interests determine by simple direct causation that they will be conservatives or advocates of reform and change. This again, is a matter usually determined by a complex of factors. Reform leaders may spring from any of these different privileged social groups, and may include military leaders, clergy, rich landowners, and men of business. Leaders of conservatism or reaction likewise have come from widely divergent backgrounds, and often not from families of wealth or position.

The easiest type to distinguish is the opportunistic adventurer, whose chief purpose is personal power. Unfortunately the political history of the Latin American nations furnishes too many examples of this type, usually thrown up in periods of political chaos, when the regular forces for maintaining law and order have broken down. Mariano Melgarejo, president and dictator of Bolivia from 1864 to 1871, is one of the clearest examples.

Lacking legitimate political objectives and having no adequate policies for the national welfare, he owed his position to the personal loyalty of his followers, to his personal courage, and to his almost complete lack of scruples in disposing of his rivals. He was ultimately overthrown by the same kind of political personalism which had brought him to power.[2] Rafael Carrera, president of Guatemala after 1839 is a similar example of an ignorant, illiterate "strong man" who sought power for its own sake. Yet he differs from Melgarejo in that he was more clearly used, at least at the beginning of his rule, by conservative landowners and clergy as an instrument for maintaining law and order. Juan Manuel Rosas, dictator of Argentina from 1835 until his overthrow in 1852, is different from both the others. Rosas was a man of keen intelligence, however limited his economic and political views may have been. He had already demonstrated not only military ability, but administrative ability as well, before assuming control of Argentina. At the outset he seems to have been motivated largely by the interests of the *estanciero* class, and during most of his rule he enjoyed great popularity in the province of Buenos Aires. But the lust for power got the better of Rosas, and his regime fell because he failed to solve the political and economic problems of national organization, and because in the inevitable course of the cycle the American spirit destroys dictatorship. This type of leader has not been included in the present volume, although it is the author's hope, sometime, to study the personal dictator in Latin America as an expression of the social and political situation of which he is a part. The type has been mentioned here, briefly, simply that the reader may have the advantage of comparing him with the types represented in the biographies which follow, and because the personal dictator has received so much attention, amounting sometimes almost to an obsession, in Latin American political thought.

POLITICAL LEADERS

Nine outstanding political leaders are described in the first part of this volume. They have been selected in part because they represent different types, but even more because of some constructive contribution to Latin American life. Some are radicals, some are moderates, some incline toward conservatism. In the main they are all men of liberal views. Some were revolutionary leaders, others were distinguished for their work in times of peace. Two were priests. One was a Negro and another (Morelos) probably was a mulatto. But all were constructive statesmen, whatever degree of success they may have achieved in carrying out their aims. All were moved by objectives which went well beyond the motives of personal power,

[2] For a vivid novelized biography of Melgarejo, see Max Daireaux, *Melgarejo, un tyran romantique*. Paris, Calman-Lévy. 1945. 284p.

and were moved by deep feelings of patriotism. All made some contribution to the development of democracy in Latin America.

Toussaint L'Ouverture, leader of the Haitian independence movement, is a characteristic product of the turbulence and violence of the slave insurrection which he led. He was a strange mixture of liberal concepts of statesmanship with primitive cunning which showed itself in secretive and overly complicated moves in politics or war. He was principally a war leader, although he displayed great qualities of statesmanship in the brief opportunity given him to rule his people in time of relative peace. Whether he overreached himself in plotting against the French authorities after accepting an armistice, or whether he was betrayed by his lieutenants to whom he gave misplaced confidence is still a question for historians to dispute. Yet he never sought power for its own sake, and his career as a whole exhibits qualities of statesmanship of a high order.

The Mexican Morelos was also the type of leader produced by a popular uprising. It is significant that he had a considerable Negro following, and that he himself was part Negro, although his family enjoyed the social status of a good creole family in Valladolid, present day Morelia. His career suggests that the role of the Negro and Negro leadership in the independence of the Americas still needs a great deal more study. Morelos was the interesting combination of priest turned soldier who gave the independence movement its first successful military leadership. That he was also a statesman is shown by his handling of the Congress and Constitution of Chilpancingo. He became the "soul of the war and the personification of the cause of independence." His defeat and capture were due in the main to external conditions over which he had no control, such as the restoration of Ferdinand in Spain. But he himself failed, perhaps because of his drastic measures, to gain the support of the substantial liberal creole elements in Mexico City which were essential to his success.

Mariano Moreno, the man of May, and Bernardino Rivadavia, the ill-starred first president of Argentina, were radical reforming leaders of that country's early history. The relative ease with which Argentine independence was maintained after 1810, and the unique position of the City and Province of Buenos Aires, which controlled the rapidly increasing revenues from foreign and interprovincial commerce, gave these men exceptional opportunities to pursue their plans of national consolidation based upon social and economic reforms. Both men combined doctrinaire characteristics with a keen sense of political realities, and both saw their plans go awry, partly, no doubt, because they failed to assess properly either the facts of the international scene or the facts of real political autonomy in the provinces.

Santander, the Colombian "man of laws," has been overshadowed by the greater figure of Bolívar. Without the divine afflatus of the Liberator, he represented a group of leaders of New Granada who, while holding republican views, opposed what they considered the more radical and extreme Bolivarian measures. They were not antirepublican. In some respects they were more ardent republicans than Bolívar, particularly in advocating a federalized, decentralized republic. But on the whole they were moderates, and their federalism, while prompted in part, of course, by the North American example, finds its chief significance in the fact that it gave greater play to local political forces which were generally conservative in character. In fact, Colombian federalism suggests many resemblances to the political realism of the authors of *The Federalist*, and to the later views of the Argentine Juan B. Alberdi. Santander, moreover, was a leader who imposed himself chiefly by the sheer force of his administrative ability. He was one of the ablest political leaders of the days of independence, a typical leader to appear in time of political crisis.

The Brazilian priest, Diogo Antônio Feijó, is another example of the kind of substantial leadership which Latin America has produced in time of political crisis. His career is also representative in many ways of the forces and conditions peculiar to nineteenth century Brazil. Though an ardent reformer, he owed his political position to the ability which he had demonstrated to take strong and effective measures for the maintenance of order and the rule of law. Although some recent Brazilian students have tried to read into his career as regent of the empire an unsuccessful experiment in republicanism, his record seems to indicate consistent adherence to the monarchical system. As regent he tried to play the role of a liberal, constitutional monarch. At the same time, his political support came from those elements of Brazilian society who wished to see rather thoroughgoing reform of government, army, church, and education. In some ways his brief career as regent gives a foretaste of the role which the liberal Emperor Pedro II was later destined to follow. Feijó's resignation was due to the gathering strength of the conservative opposition, which was concerned with a defense of the institution of slavery. His downfall seems to have meant the postponement of moderate reform in Brazil for several decades.

Balmaceda and Irigoyen typify the new vigorous leadership which became so marked around the turn of the century, first in Chile and subsequently in Argentina. Both were leaders of a new type indicative of the broadening base of popular participation in the political life of the nation. The analogies are admittedly superficial, but the student of the political history of the United States cannot fail to see a certain resemblance to the leadership of Andrew Jackson, or even more particularly in the case of Irigoyen, to William Jennings Bryan. Irigoyen was a great party leader, and he owed his unique and highly personal political power largely to his adroit control of elements of popular unrest through the effective operation of the Radical Party, a party which was to a large extent his own creation.

Though there is more of the element of *noblesse oblige* about Balmaceda, he shows the same popular appeal to the working classes in opposition to the ruling oligarchy. The constitutional conflict in which his career culminated somewhat obscures the real issue, for it gave the new conservative grouping formed in opposition to him the opportunity to defend what is usually considered the liberal position of parliamentary supremacy. The true significance of his liberal leadership, however, as will be seen, lies in the fact that his suicide, while it came out of the frustration of defeat and was partly motivated by the desire to protect his party lieutenants, became to many Spanish Americans a powerful symbol of liberalism and reform in the years which followed.

Both Balmaceda and Irigoyen belong spiritually to the generation of political leadership of Francisco Madero and José Batlle. While they were liberal reformers, their interest centered in the achievement of a more democratic political structure. However, both succeeded, perhaps in large measure unintentionally, as did Madero and Batlle, in defining more clearly the fundamental issues of underlying social and economic reform. Both were overthrown by a new grouping of conservative forces fearful of the extent to which the popular tendencies might go.

Ruy Barbosa of Brazil belongs to the same generation. But Brazilian leadership, and this is true of his case, shows peculiar traits of its own. His greatest achievement lay in the moral leadership he exerted—his bold defense of the rights of the political victims of the dictatorship of Marshall Peixoto, and his aggressive opposition to the threat of militarism represented in the presidential candidacy of General Hermes de Fonseca. He believed that "material facts emanate from moral facts," and his career was an exemplification of this belief. A moral crusader, suggestive of Woodrow Wilson, he never let himself become a revolutionist, even when that course might possibly have won him the presidency of his country.

LEADERS OF THOUGHT

The second half of this volume is devoted to seven men who have shaped the development of thought in Latin America. They are all men well known to Latin American students, but all too little known north of the Rio Grande. *Pensadores* or men of ideas have occupied a very prominent place in Latin American life. On the whole, they have exercised more influence, directly or indirectly, on the movements of politics than have their counterparts in the United States. A whole political generation in Chile followed the ideas of the *maestro*, Andrés Bello, and almost all the present political leadership of Latin America has had its ideas profoundly colored by the poet Darío, the sociologist-psychologist Ingenieros, the

philosophers Enrique Rodó and Antonio Caso, or others of their kind.
Hence the author has thought that a book dealing with political leaders
should also give a prominent place to the men who gave those leaders many
of their ideas, suggesting and helping to form the courses of action which
they followed.

As in the case of the political leaders there is a wide range of types
among the men of ideas. Indeed, one may find among them almost any
variety of thought which has been present in Western civilization during
the past century and a half. The seven men selected for discussion were
chosen because they happen to represent various distinctive elements which
have entered into the making of the Latin American mind and because they
illustrate the variety of its manifestations. They are not presented as the
seven most important thinkers of Latin America, although several of them
well deserve that distinction. Measured by the yardstick of radicalism and
conservatism they would extend over a wide gamut. They differ at least
as much as they agree. If they have one trait in common it is a certain
note of fundamental optimism, probably a characteristic of the New World.

To understand the significance and influence of these men who have
guided the thinking of Latin America it is necessary, of course, to know
something of the tendencies in its intellectual development since independence. Yet it would be out of place here to attempt to describe this development in any detail. It is, in fact, quite doubtful whether it could be done
in any very satisfying fashion, since the necessary groundwork has not been
done by scholars working in the field. The best work in English, by Professor W. Rex Crawford, is little more than a sketch of the main ideas of
some of the outstanding thinkers, with little effort to develop a synthesis
of the developments as a whole. Several Latin Americans have recently
treated various special phases of the subject.[3] But until the larger task has
been done it is very difficult to write with any degree of assurance upon
the historical tendencies of Latin American thought.

A few general characteristics may be mentioned, however. Although,
as one might expect, Latin American thought has a number of American
aspects, still, it has followed European patterns in general. Thought of the
early nineteenth century reflected that of the North American and French
Revolutions, with its backgrounds in the seventeenth and eighteenth century
thought of Locke, Montesquieu, Rousseau, Smith, the French Encyclopedists
and Moralists, and such early nineteenth century writers as Godwin and
Bentham. These ideas continued to influence the writers of national histories
and the students of international law pretty well up to the present day. The
last half of the nineteenth century reflected the growth of scientific and

[3] Crawford, W. Rex. *A Century of Latin-American Thought*. Cambridge, Harvard University Press. 1944. 320p; Poviña, Alfredo. *Historia de la sociología latino-americana*. México,
Fondo de Cultura Económica. 1941. 236p; Gondra, Luis Roque and others. *El pensamiento
económico latino-americano*. México, Fondo de Cultura Económica. 1945. 333p.

evolutionary thought in Europe and the United States. The ideas of Darwin, Spencer, and Comte had the greatest impact, but almost every European tendency found its counterpart in the Latin American scene. One of the outstanding developments of this period was the appearance in the law faculties of the Latin American universities of courses in national or American sociology in which a philosophical and historical approach was made to national problems of almost every character. Many books were published on this theme.

The Spanish "Generation of '98" also found a lively reflection in America and helped stimulate a vigorous and varied growth of Latin American thought after the turn of the century. French influence was particularly strong, with Taine, Bergson, Boutroux and Meyerson giving way in the twentieth century to Jacques Maritain. German idealists, such as George Christian Krause, had their day, while the vogue of Dilthey, Spengler, Weber, Simmel, Husserl, and Heidegger lent itself to a sociological approach to problems of knowledge. German influences frequently found their way into Latin America by way of the writings of the Spanish philosopher, Ortega y Gasset. Another Spaniard, Unamuno, also achieved an important influence. Increasing contact with education in the United States brought a noticeable contribution from William James and John Dewey. Strong Marxian tendencies also appeared, as in the works of the Argentine Alfredo Palacios, the Cuban Juan Marinello, the Peruvian Carlos Mariátegui, and many others. On the whole, however, the twentieth century shows less slavish following of European models, and more distinctively American traits. The tendency to look in the American scene for the roots of American thought finds more frequent and stronger expression. Thought is more nationalistic and at the same time more concerned with international questions. It has an increasing note of American self-confidence and of American idealism and optimism.

While it is hoped that the seven thinkers presented here will suggest something of the great influence which intellectuals have exercised upon social and political activity and upon the formation of national culture, it should be borne in mind that seven men cannot adequately portray the wide variety of the thought of twenty nations. A practical consideration also operated to restrict the field of choice. Since some of the greatest leaders of thought in Latin America have been political leaders as well, a number of them have been discussed in the first section of this book, as well as in the author's previous *Makers of Democracy in Latin America.*[4] Certainly any list which aims at completeness would include Bolívar, Monteagudo, Sarmiento, Alberdi, Mitre, Martí, González Prada and Mariátegui, who were discussed in that volume, as well as Moreno and Ruy Barbosa discussed

⁴ Davis, Harold E. *Makers of Democracy in Latin America.* New York, H. W. Wilson Company. 1945. 124p. (Inter-American Bibliographical and Library Association. Publications. Series I, vol. 9)

as political leaders in this one. It would also deal with many others: Francisco Bilbao and Benjamín Vicuña Mackenna of Chile, Carlos Vaz Ferreira and Alberto Zum Felde of Uruguay; Ernesto Quesada, Carlos Bunge, Alejandro Korn, Manuel Gálvez, and Ricardo Rojas of Argentina; Benjamin Constant, Ivan Mario Lins, Gilberto Freyre, and Fernando de Azevedo of Brazil; Félix Varela, Enrique José Varona, Eugenio María de Hostos, and Fernando Ortiz of Cuba; Justo Sierra and Samuel Ramos of Mexico; Luis Alberto Sánchez and Alejandro O. Deústua of Peru—and still the list would not be complete.

The *pensador*, or man of ideas, is an important and recognizable type everywhere in Latin America. His thought is comprehensive and global. He touches upon the widest range of subjects, from immediate political questions to the most abstruse problems of philosophy. He frequently combines history with sociology, politics, economics, ethics and literary criticism or esthetics. Of the seven men treated in the following pages, Antonio Caso, José Ingenieros, Andrés Bello and, possibly, José Enrique Rodó may be taken as representative of this type. This holds true, even though Rodó and Bello are usually thought of first for their contributions to belles lettres, or in the case of Bello, for his work on the Spanish language and grammar. The others represent various and different types, all characteristic of the Latin American intellectual scene, however. Fernández de Lizardi was a pamphleteer and one of the founders of Mexican national literature. Da Cunha was a journalist who happened to write Brazil's greatest book, almost as if by accident. Rubén Darío was a strange combination of diplomat and bohemian poet, yet represents one of the strongest intellectual forces of them all.

Lizardi found himself in the dilemma of many creoles of his time in Mexico. He believed in independence and was convinced that it should be accompanied by thoroughgoing social and political reforms. But the excesses of the first insurrectionaries frightened him, and he vacillated and hesitated to join the movement openly after seeing the violence in which Hidalgo's turbulent mass of Indian, mestizo, and Negro followers engaged. A tortured soul who expressed in writing what he could not express in action, he sharpened the edge of the Mexican protest against the political injustice and the social and cultural repression of Spanish rule. His pen name, *El Pensador Mexicano*, struck the keynote of Americanism which characterized all his ideas and their influence.

Andrés Bello was the broadest scholar of them all—a titan who seemed to shape the life of early Chile by the sheer weight of his intellect and his great erudition. Poet, literary critic, jurist, diplomat, grammarian and educator, no matter to which activity or literary form he turned his hand, he left some great achievement, and inspired followers to carry on the task of "civilizing" Chile.

The fact of having written the great book of a nation is sufficient to give Euclides da Cunha of Brazil an honored place in his nation's hall of fame. But even more significant than the popularity and the literary qualities of *Os Sertões* (The Backlands) was the fact that da Cunha discovered to his fellow countrymen something of the sociological as well as the biological basis of the people and culture which were evolving into the Brazilian nation. He was not entirely happy about the mongrel racial type which had grown up in the backlands, the *Sertanejo*, or man of the backlands, for he subscribed in part to Gobineau's ideas of superior and "pure" races. Yet he saw in the *Sertanejo* the new American basis of Brazilian nationality. He described what he saw as a faithful reporter, and the luminous picture which he drew left an indelible impression on the minds of Brazilians.

As the greatest poet of his age in Spanish America, Rubén Darío had a great influence in shaping the mind and spirit of a whole generation of Latin Americans. The music of his verse left its stamp upon people of all walks of life, while his spirit of rebellion, profoundly American in spite of his sympathy with the French modernists, was a spiritual tonic to Latin American youth of the turn of the century in its search for self-confidence to overcome the political frustrations of the age.

The cool Olympic tones of José Enrique Rodó, and his dispassionate aloofness, cause him to stand out among Latin American authors. Yet his quiet appeal for idealism to guide and shape a Latin America which was being transformed rapidly by material prosperity and European immigration struck a sympathetic note, especially among young people. It was strange indeed that a man who appeared morbidly timid should become the idol of university youths, inspiring them to emulate his quiet courage. Yet there was also an element of estheticism—an element of escapism—about Rodó and his ideas which has left its mark on the intellectuals of Latin America today, many of whom still highly esteem his writings.

In striking contrast Ingenieros, the author of *Mediocre Man*, was a turbulent, insouciant spirit, who led student demonstrations and engaged in hilarious escapades and practical jokes during his student days, and who seemed never to have lost his penchant for robust humor. He was unmatched in his day for the vigor with which he devoted himself to the solution of the social and intellectual problems of Argentina and of the modern world. This son of an Italian immigrant became thoroughly American in spirit, and the greatest contribution of his life was the ringing appeal to Latin American youth, in his *Mediocre Man*, to rise above the limitations of their environment and of what he considered to be the debasing materialism and indifference of their day.

The title of *maestro* is an accolade of great distinction in Latin America, bestowed by devoted students upon men whose intellectual influence in the universities has been particularly significant. Antonio Caso well deserved this distinction. His "personalist" and humanistic philosophy represents one of the strong tendencies in contemporary thought in Latin America. He owes a great debt to European thought—to Bergson and Meyerson among others. Yet an American attitude of independence and, perhaps, an influence of William James may be seen in his refusal to be bound to any "system" of thought. Fundamentally a humanist, and conservative, he placed great weight on the individual's finding his complete personal development in the culture of which he is a part, and upon the idea of an intellectual elite. Consequently, he showed considerable sympathy for the philosophy of culture underlying fascism and National Socialism in their early stages. He was distressed by the "materialism" and by the lack of a positive cultural and spiritual affirmation in democracy and communism. Yet he never took up with neo-Thomism, as might have been expected, and never went to the lengths that Manuel Gálvez of Argentina went in embracing the doctrines of Franco's *Hispanidad*.[5] As the fascist systems began to display more and more tyrranical aspects, to the point where they seemed bent upon crushing all individual liberty, he turned again, as so many other Latin American intellectuals did, to an ardent defense of democracy. Perhaps this was just another instance of the triumph of the American spirit.

Both the political leaders and the leaders of thought have been arranged in chronological sequence so that the reader may get some sense of changing emphases and directions during the course of a century and a half of developments. But the reader must be warned again at this point not to assume that this series of sketches is in any sense intended as a balanced history of political developments or of the intellectual history of Latin America. The author will be happy if he has led the reader to some additional insight into certain aspects of the problems of Latin American civilization and the way in which political and intellectual leaders have approached their solution.

Suggestions for further reading have been placed at the end of each sketch. These are not intended as complete bibliographies. The best works available in English have been suggested, and one or more studies by Latin Americans, usually the ones which the author has found most helpful for his own understanding of the subject.

[5] See Bailey Diffie, "The Ideology of Hispanidad." *Hispanic American Historical Review.* 23:457-82. August 1943.

Part I

POLITICAL LEADERS

TOUSSAINT L'OUVERTURE (1743?-1803)

LEADER OF AMERICAN NEGRO LIBERATION

The history of the movement for independence in Latin America has no more dramatic story than that of the former slave, Toussaint L'Ouverture,[1] the inspired leader of the uprising of Negroes in Haiti which brought about that country's independence. It is hard to view dispassionately the leader of a slave insurrection, and the literature on Toussaint and the Haitian revolution is more than full of contradictions. Sometimes he is presented as the simple tool of scheming white leaders and foreign political interests. At the opposite extreme he is represented as a scheming, relentless Machiavellian political and military leader, whose only object was personal power. From the standpoint of the United States, a fair evaluation and sympathetic understanding of the great Haitian leader is all the more difficult because of the effects which the Haitian revolution had upon public opinion of the time. The slave-owning class, especially, became obsessed with the fear of slave insurrection after the successful example had been set in Haiti. Even today, North American historians of American independence movements are curiously obtuse to the significance of the fact that the first nation of Latin America to follow the revolutionary example of the United States was a Negro republic.

The French colony of Saint Domingue, or modern Haiti,[2] occupied the western third of the island of Santo Domingo or Hispaniola, the site of the oldest colony of Spain in America. French buccaneers had first settled on the small island of Tortuga, off the northwest coast, about 1625. Shortly afterward they moved into the largely unoccupied western end of Hispaniola. Then by the Treaty of Ryswick in 1697 France acquired title to the western part of the island from Spain. The remainder of the island was Spanish Santo Domingo, the modern Dominican Republic. It was sparsely settled and largely pastoral in economy. French Saint Domingue, on the other hand, while it had developed slowly at first, by the middle of the eighteenth century had become a flourishing center of coffee, cotton, indigo, and sugar plantations. Population and wealth grew rapidly. The prosperous sugar plantations, especially, supported a wealthy planter class which had come to prominence in French society.

At the end of the eighteenth century French Haiti, or Saint Domingue, had a popuation of a little over a half million persons. Of these less than

[1] Or Louverture. This name or title was probably adopted by Toussaint or attributed to him on the basis of passages in voodoo which refer to the "Opener" of the way to destiny.
[2] Haiti is the aboriginal name of the island. It persisted in popular use under Spanish and French rule and was revived and officially adopted by independent Haiti in 1804.

10 per cent were white, but they were the principal land owners. There were some 450,000 Negro slaves and some 28,000 free persons of color, largely mulattoes. The development of sugar plantations was especially rapid after 1750, and, as a result, a large part of the slaves were first generation immigrants. The relatively large number of free mulattoes was due in part to a law of Louis XIV which declared children of mixed marriages free. But in the last half of the eighteenth century the precarious position of a rich planter class in the midst of a rapidly growing slave population was reflected in increasingly rigid discriminatory legislation and closer drawing of racial lines in general. The white planters grew wealthier and more arrogant. The envy of the poor whites increased, while both groups became increasingly apprehensive of the freedmen. A spirit of quarrelsomeness developed among these groups which boded ill in the event of a slave uprising.

The French Revolution set loose in Haiti the most explosive social revolution of the entire American independence movment. It was a revolution which developed in two main streams. The first was a movement of the freed Negroes and mulattoes, and centered in the southern and western parts of the colony. Its objective was to win the rights of French citizens, including participation in elections and membership in a colonial assembly, for their class. The second was a slave insurrection which centered in the northern part of the colony, where the largest and richest sugar plantations were located. This was the movement of which Toussaint L'Ouverture ultimately became the leader.

In 1789, when the Estates General met in France, the Haitian planters had sent delegates, against the wish of the governor of the island. These colonial delegates had tried to secure approval of political arrangements for Saint Domingue which would exclude the free Negroes and mulattoes. This effort failed because of the opposition of the French anti-slavery society, *Les Amis des Noires*. The wealthy mulattoes also presented their case to the Estates General, accompanied by the sum of $1,200,000 and a promise to donate a fifth of their wealth toward paying the national debt. But the planters went ahead to assemble a constitutional convention which met under their domination at St. Marc's the following year. Although it made minor concessions to the freedmen, and proposed to revise the slave codes, this assembly, moved partly by the desire to prevent any interference with slavery in the island, devoted itself chiefly to securing the right of the colony to control its own affairs independent of the Assembly in France.

Meanwhile a revolt of free Negroes and mulattoes broke out, led by Vincent Ogé, a wealthy mulatto planter and friend of Robespierre. Behind the Ogé uprising, which took place in the north, around Le Cap, lay the play of complicated rivalries and jealousies among white planters, poor whites, and the French officials, as well as the discontent of the mulattoes.

Ogé had considered arming a slave revolt, but had decided against it. His uprising was suppressed. He escaped across the border into Spanish territory, but was surrendered to the French colonial authorities and executed with great cruelty.

In May of 1791 the French National Assembly, exasperated by the conduct of the white planters, approved a new decree establishing the rights of the free colored people of Haiti and called for a new colonial assembly, in which the freedmen should be represented. The whites prepared to resist this law, and the governor took no steps to uphold it. Feeling that they had been betrayed, the free Negroes and mulattoes of the south and west revolted. This revolt, led by André Rigaud, was short-lived, for the whites in the west, frightened by the slave insurrection which had broken out in the north four days before, quickly reached an agreement with the mulatto leaders. This agreement provided that the garrison of Port-au-Prince, the capital, should be composed of both white and Negro troops. It condemned the execution of Ogé, and provided for a new colonial assembly elected in conformity with the decree of the French National Assembly. The plantation owners were now able to secure cooperation of many free Negroes and mulattoes in opposing the slave insurrection.

Two years of agitation in the colony had created great unrest among the Negro slaves. Ogé became a martyr, and his execution seemed to be the spark necessary to set off a widespread revolt. Some historians have claimed that it was white leaders who instigated the insurrection, in the hope that suppression of a slave uprising would confirm white control of the island, and some evidence suggests a Spanish interest in the Negro revolt. The fact that the followers of Toussaint called themselves royalists until 1793 might seem to give some color to the claim, but this can be explained on other grounds, as will be noted. It has also been blamed variously on the mulattoes and on white abolitionists or other revolutionists newly arrived from France. On the whole, the claim of white inspiration is hard to believe, and has never been well proved. It seems much more reasonable to assume that the instigation came from the Negroes themselves.

On August 14, 1791, a secret meeting of slave leaders was held to plan the insurrection. On the night of August 22 the full fury of the rebellion broke forth. Plans had been well laid, for the attacks on the white planters began almost simultaneously throughout the province. Houses were burned and white men, women, and children were killed indiscriminately. All the resources of savage minds were drawn upon to devise new and more excruciating forms of torture and death. Gangs of slaves roamed the countryside with the heads of white children fixed on their pikes. Nor did the whites fail to retaliate with the same kind of violence against captured Negroes. Although not its first leader, it was Toussaint L'Ouverture who first proved able to control this insurrectionary violence, and to give it purpose and direction: independence and emancipation.

François Dominique Toussaint was born about 1743 on the Breda plantation in northern Haiti, a few miles from Cap Haitien. His father and mother, both of the Arada tribe, had been brought to Haiti from Africa as slaves. His father, whom some of Toussaint's biographers claim to have been a chieftain or the son of a chief in Africa, was known for his knowledge of medicinal herbs, a knowledge which Toussaint later acquired. His mother died when Toussaint was a small boy.

As a slave boy he was put to work as soon as he was old enough to watch the flocks of sheep and goats on the Breda plantation. He was a small child, and as he himself was accustomed to remark, ugly and ill-shaped, a "fratras baton" or crooked stick. Yet he learned to excel in swimming and horseback riding. As he grew older he was employed as a herder and developed a great liking for horses. Somehow he acquired the rudiments of an education, probably from his godfather, who had been instructed by a Jesuit missionary before the expulsion of the order from the island. Or perhaps he was taught by his father—the record is not clear. He spoke the Arada language, which many of the slaves spoke, and the Creole, or corrupted French patois of the island. He never learned to write or speak French correctly, and his secretaries later struggled to turn his effective but ungrammatical language into correct form.

The Breda plantation was known throughout the island for the generous treatment of its slaves. Its owner was the Count de Noe, living in France. The manager was Bayon de Libertat, to whose family Toussaint developed a strong attachment. Libertat discovered the ability of Toussaint, encouraged him in his study, and later advanced him to positions of responsibility, so that he eventually became manager of the plantation sugar mill. We know that during these years he had developed his knowledge of French and had read a number of books, including Caesar's *Commentaries* and the *Histoire philosophique et politique des établissements et du commerce des Européens dan les deux Indes* of the Abbé Raynal, who influenced so many of the Latin American revolutionary leaders. He must have read there those striking words: "The Negroes lack but a chief. Where is the great man? He will appear; we have no doubt of it. He will show himself; he will unfurl the sacred standard of liberty."

He married, at the age of twenty-five, a good-natured Negress named Suzanne Simon, who was to be his faithful companion until his exile to France separated them. Suzanne had a son, Placide, by a mulatto, but Toussaint adopted him and brought him up as his own. The fact that Toussaint was married with a church ceremony indicates clearly that he had achieved a position well above that of the ordinary slaves, for whom such formalities were rarely used. He and Suzanne had several children of their own, and Toussaint was always a devoted father, giving time and attention to the education of his children, even in the midst of his campaigns.

Toussaint was of medium height, and with the years acquired a dignified grave appearance. He had the thick lips, the broad flat nose, and the wide nostrils of the Negro, and a stubborn projecting jaw. His coal black eyes flashed animation, kindness, or anger according to his mood. The tone of his voice was nasal and high-pitched. His hair was brushed straight back from his forehead in a queue, in the French manner.

Although he was aware of the developments, and may even have participated to some extent in the early meeting which led to the insurrection, Toussaint took no active part at first, and slaves on the Breda plantation stayed at their tasks. Finally, when the revolt had spread throughout the north, he saw the Libertat family off safely to Le Cap (Cap Haitien), sent his own wife and family across the border into Spanish Santo Domingo, and deliberately joined the revolutionary forces. Most of the Breda slaves did likewise.

The first leader of the slave insurrection was Boukman, a former slave from Jamaica, but he was soon captured and executed. Command was then taken over by three leaders: Biassou, Jean François and Jeannott. The latter, who was guilty of the most violent excesses, was soon killed by the Negroes. Biassou and Jean François were thus left in command. At first they were suspicious of Toussaint, because of his education, because of his not joining the rebellion at first, and because of the care with which he had guarded the Libertats. They therefore refused to give him a military command, although he deserved it because of the number of Breda slaves he had brought with him. He was assigned instead to medical duties. But his ability soon made itself felt and he became aide to Biassou with the rank of brigadier general.

The Negroes adopted the cause of the French king, using the white Bourbon standard. The white planters in the north, meanwhile, had appealed to the governor of English Jamaica for aid, and had adopted the British colors in an act of defiance of the French authorities. The Governor of Jamaica refused to send military assistance at this time, but did assist many of the planters to escape from the island. Many of the whites stayed on and took an active part in later developments. When the whites saw the Negroes using the Bourbon standard they immediately suspected that French counter-revolutionaries had spread the rumor that King Louis XVI was in danger from the Revolutionary government in France because he was in favor of Negro emancipation.

Meanwhile, a commission from the French National Assembly had reached the island. They did their best to end the slave insurrection. They met with the Negro leaders and reached an agreement with them, near the end of 1791. But the Colonial Assembly refused to approve the agreement, and the commissioners left, having failed to achieve their object of pacifying the colony. A second commission arrived late in 1792 supported by a strong fleet and an army of 6,000 troops. They were instructed to end the strife between the factions by securing a general agreement to recognize the political rights of the freedmen. The commissioners proclaimed that henceforth there were to be but two classes of persons in the colony: citizens without distinction of color, and slaves. It soon became clear, however, that there was little hope of achieving their objective of uniting all the factions in opposition to the Negro uprising. Instead, they seemed to stir up more trouble between the planters and the poor whites.

As if to complicate matters further, a French governor and military commander now appeared at Le Cap who took sides with the white planters against the commission. The commissioners led an army of whites and mulattoes into Le Cap and forced Governor Galbaud to withdraw, but he soon returned with two thousand troops and defeated the commissioners. The latter retaliated by opening the gates of the city to a band of Negroes who pillaged the town and forced Galbaud out again. The commissioners now retired to the mountains. They had lost hope of reconciling the white planters, and shortly issued a proclamation offering freedom to all the slaves who would join forces with them. Biassou, Toussaint, and Jean François rejected this offer. They still maintained their royalist position and suspected that the republican authorities were the tools of the white planters who would reenslave them.

Yet, on the whole, the French forces were making progress in gaining control of the colony when news of the execution of the French monarch reached the island in the spring of 1793. Spain and England soon went to war against France with nearly disastrous results in Haiti. The Colonial Assembly, representing the white planters, reached an agreement with the Governor of Jamaica, and a fleet of twenty-two English vessels appeared off the coast and began to occupy the principal ports of the island. The Negro leaders, still maintaining their position as "royalists," joined forces with the authorities of Spanish Santo Domingo, who promised them freedom. The Negroes still did not trust the proclamation of complete emancipation issued by Commissioner Sonthonox, on his sole authority, on August 29, 1793.

Toussaint took with him a force of six hundred well trained and well armed men, and received a Spanish commission as brigadier general. Most of the Spanish victories which followed were due to his leadership. Soon he was joined by a number of French officers from Galbaud's forces, who fled to Spanish Santo Domingo after the defeat at Le Cap. His Negro army of four thousand men was known as the best trained and the best cared-for in the Spanish island forces. Operating from Spanish territory, he carried out a series of successful moves. He captured Marmelade, Ennery, Plaisance, and Gonaïves, forcing several republican bands to surrender. Some of them joined his forces. As a result of Toussaint's exploits the Spanish had established control over most of north Haiti and considerable parts of the south and the west by the end of 1793.

The British had occupied most of the western coast, and were at the point of capturing Port-au-Prince. Wherever they went they restored order and Negro slavery (as they also did in the French islands of Martinique and Guadeloupe). In the north the French republican General Laveaux held out at great odds against the Spanish and English, and in the south there was Rigaud, the mulatto leader. At this point, in February 1794, the French Assembly confirmed the decree abolishing slavery, and Toussaint came to the conclusion that he would best further the cause of Negro emancipation by joining forces with the French republicans. In May he came to terms with General Laveaux, who had been sustaining a desperate siege at Port de Paix, raised the republican flag, and led an army of four thousand men to Laveaux's relief. Laveaux was to remain his lifelong friend. The French commission, which had been ready in desperation to return to France, decided to remain. Within fifteen days the Spaniards were forced to give up all their Haitian territory, and the combined Negro and republican forces were free to move against the English. Jean François and Biassou remained with the Spaniards. Toussaint defeated them, and they took no further important part in Haitian history.

Toussaint now cooperated with the mulatto General Rigaud (later to be his bitter enemy) in a drive against the English. By the end of 1795 the latter had been driven from most of the island except Port-au-Prince. In that year Spain returned to her alliance with France and Spanish Santo Domingo was transferred by agreement to the French.[3] Thus, within less than two years, a complete change had been brought about in the military and political situation in the island. French authority had been reestablished, largely because of the decisive actions of Toussaint and his Negro army.

General Laveaux had assumed the position of governor-general, but his appointment was not confirmed in France. A new commissioner, who was none other than General Hédouville, the famous pacificator of the Vendée, forced him to return to France. But Hédouville was to learn quickly that the real power in the island lay not in the hands of the French authorities, but in those of General Rigaud with his mulatto cavalry and of Toussaint with his loyal army of ex-slaves. Toussaint was gathering around

[3] Spanish Santo Domingo was returned to Spain in 1814.

him such leaders as Henri Christophe and Dessalines, both destined to play prominent roles in the later history of Haiti, and his prestige was rapidly growing beyond that of any other leader in the island. When General Laveaux had been threatened by an insurrection at Le Cap, Toussaint threatened to attack the city and secured the general's liberation by issuing orders to the insurrectionists that he should be set free. From that point on there could be no serious question that Toussaint was the real ruler of the island.

That this was true became even clearer when the English General Maitland finally evacuated Port-au-Prince and capitulated in the year 1798. He insisted upon surrendering to Toussaint L'Ouverture, much to the annoyance of the French commissioner. When a new French commissioner, Roume, arrived shortly thereafter, there was little that he could do except to cooperate with Toussaint.

During the next two years, from 1798 to 1800, civil war broke out between Rigaud and Toussaint, ending in victory for the latter. During this war sometimes one and sometimes the other seemed to have the support of French Commissioner Roume, but the latter was powerless to control the war. Edward Stevens, the United States representative in Haiti, was carrying on conversations at this time with Toussaint concerning the opening of trade with the United States. He wrote on February 18, 1798 that "everything announces a speedy dissolution of those ties which once connected this important colony with the mother country." He also reported that Toussaint was being urged by the French government to plan expeditions against the United States and against British possessions in the Caribbean. Trade with Great Britain and the United States was in fact opened by a secret agreement in 1799, signed by Toussaint and a British representative. This agreement stilled the immediate fear of Negro invasion of the United States or British possessions. However, Napoleon had said that unless Toussaint were overthrown the scepter of the New World would sooner or later pass into the hands of the blacks, and there were many in the United States who were coming to be of the same mind.

Napoleon had now come to power in France and was determined to revive the French empire in America. Whether or not he was opposed in principle to the rule of the Negroes in the colony of Haiti, he determined to end once and for all the chaos and disorder which had reigned during the last years. His plan was to send an expeditionary force so overwhelming that there could be no question of its success. As leader of the expedition he chose General Leclerc, husband of the somewhat wayward Pauline Bonaparte. Napoleon's younger brother, Jerome, accompanied the expedition. With it also went the two sons of Toussaint, Placide and Isaac, who had been in a military school in France. They were taken as hostages, and were supposed to help reconcile the father to the authority of the French Republic.

The French historian, Thiers, speaking of the situation at this time, credits Toussaint with great political intelligence and asserts that he had shown true genius in reestablishing life in Haiti. He had subdued a revolted people, wrote Thiers, and had established a government over them. He had stopped the Negroes from killing each other and from killing the whites, and had reestablished agriculture and commerce. In fact, he says, "in 1801, after ten years of commotion, the soil of Santo Domingo, drenched with so much blood, presented an appearance of fertility nearly equal to that which it exhibited in 1789." Thiers was not otherwise favorable in his judgments upon the Negro revolution in Haiti, so that his judgment of Toussaint is especially notable.

Peace and prosperity had indeed been reestablished before the expedition of Leclerc landed on the island with twenty thousand men supported by more than thirty ships. The Haiti of Toussaint was at peace with itself, but that did not mean it could turn back a European army. When General Rochambeau's division landed and captured Fort Dauphin, the Haitians under Henri Christophe set fire to the town and retired with their forces to the mountains. Much the same reception was given to the landing forces at Port-au-Prince, and elsewhere in the island. The thorough and stubborn resistance which Toussaint and his followers offered to the representatives of France at this time shows either that they were now determined to maintain independence or that they were convinced that this expedition was sent to put an end to the liberty which the Negroes enjoyed and to restore the institution of slavery. Probably it was the latter, since Toussaint knew that the final plan of Napoleon for Haiti, as embodied in the instructions to Leclerc, called for the reestablishment of slavery.

Toussaint had at his disposal an army of about sixteen thousand men. The invading army, as noted, numbered in the neighborhood of twenty thousand. The Haitian forces were scattered throughout the island, however, and Toussaint was never able to bring together a defensive force of more than about eight thousand. The French were immediately successful, therefore, in establishing themselves in most of the large populated places, while the Haitians took refuge in the mountains. This did not mean an end to their resistance.

In fact by May 1802, when Toussaint determined to surrender to the French leaders, the forces of Leclerc had been so far decimated that they were virtually at the mercy of the Negro leaders. Toussaint knew that Napoleon's instructions to Leclerc had been to come to terms if possible with Toussaint and his men, and then to arrest them and deport them to France. A recent biographer of Toussaint has argued convincingly, therefore, that

Toussaint, knowing these instructions, reasoned that he was strong enough and that Leclerc's white forces were sufficiently weakened for him to rely upon Leclerc's having need of him and the Negro army.[4] Toussaint's plan was to have all the Negro soldiers join Leclerc's army, to wait a few months more until yellow fever had still further decimated French ranks, and then to step in, assume command of the army, arrest Leclerc, and send him back to France.

Whether or not this was true, Toussaint's surrender did not mean his final withdrawal from the resistance movement. But it was more difficult to organize this resistance than he had expected. The events surrounding his surrender weakened his position more than he had anticipated. Christophe allowed his ambitions to get the better of him and arranged a separate agreement with Leclerc prior to Toussaint's final surrender. For this Toussaint never forgave him. Because Dessalines had been so violent in his treatment of the whites, Leclerc refused at first to accept his submission and only did so when Toussaint made it an unalterable condition of his own surrender. In spite of this evidence of loyalty, it seems clear that Dessalines, too, was disloyal to his chief, and that Toussaint's subsequent arrest by Leclerc was a result of Dessalines' betrayal.

Toussaint surrendered upon assurance that he would be allowed to retire in peace and that the Negro troops would be brigaded into the Haitian army. The treaty of May 5, 1802 with Leclerc guaranteed the liberty of all citizens of Haiti and provided that all civil and military officers should retain their offices and grades. It gave to Toussaint and his staff the right to retire to whatever part of the Haitian territory they chose.

He went to his home for a while, biding his time. He felt certain that it was only a matter of time until Leclerc's actions would bring the outbreak of further resistance. He knew also, of course, that Leclerc's instructions called for his own arrest and deportation, which could not long be delayed. Somehow, he hoped to beat the French leader to the draw, but his chance never came. On June 8, 1802, he was invited by General Burnet to come to his home to discuss arrangements for some of the discontented Negro troops. Here he was arrested on Leclerc's orders, and was immediately placed on board a French warship, with his wife, his sons, and several officers of his staff, to be sent to France. Arriving in France July 21, 1802, he was imprisoned in Fort Joux in the Jura mountains, where he remained, without trial, until his death on April 7, 1803.

On leaving Haiti Toussaint had said to his captors: "In overthrowing me, you have broken down only the trunk of the tree of liberty for the blacks; it will spring up again from its roots which are many and deep." His words were a vivid prophecy of the terrible events to follow.

[4] Korngold, Ralph. *Citizen Toussaint.* Boston, Little, Brown & Co. 1914. p283ff.

Leclerc proceeded to reform the government of Haiti so as to place the principal authority in the officers of the European army which he had brought with him, even though he continued to make use of the Haitian generals, Henri Christophe and Dessalines, who had surrendered and who still held their military rank. As he wrote back to France, he anticipated some difficulty as a result of the deportation of Toussaint. But he was not prepared for the bursting flame of insurrection which broke out shortly after Toussaint's departure—an insurrection fed and strengthened by reports that slavery had been reestablished in the islands of Guadeloupe and Martinique.

Ever since European forces had arrived in Haiti, they had suffered from the ravages of yellow fever and other tropical diseases. As the European army became weaker, Leclerc moved to disarm the black soldiers. It was this move which set off the new revolt which was soon to bring complete independence under the leadership of Dessalines and Henri Christophe, for no Negro could forget the famous words of Toussaint who, in placing a gun in the hands of a Negro soldier, had said: "This gun is your liberty."

Toussaint was the product of the violence and unrest of his times. He was not the exponent of great ideas, not a leader of thought. He represented the unformulated, unrationalized impulses of a people aroused from slavery by the impact of great social and historical forces. The Haitian Revolution was the first step in the American Negro slave's assertion of his rightful place in the New World to which he had been brought by force. A century of conflict and mounting racial tension was to follow before the process of Negro liberation would be completed. But Toussaint had become the symbol of this dawning struggle, as he had been the personification of its first and most violent phase in Haiti. His appearance on the political scene of America thus marks an epoch in the history of the Negroes in the Western Hemisphere.

The movement for Haitian independence pointed out clearly the dangers of a democratic revolution which fell into the hands of ignorant people unaccustomed to assuming the responsibilities of government, and the people of the United States quickly began to look askance at this unexpected product of the revolutionary movement which they had begun in the Western Hemisphere. White plantation owners escaping to Charleston and New Orleans from the horrors of the civil war in Haiti recounted their tales of cruelty, destruction, and disorder to the willing ears of slaveowners in South Carolina and Louisiana. This threat presented in a nearby, independent Negro republic, directed by erstwhile Negro slaves, thus played no small part in developing the aggressive and militant attitude of southern political leaders in the United States who were soon to be aroused to a defense of the "peculiar institution" of the South. What had happened in Haiti they argued might well happen in democratic United States. The example of Haiti, likewise imbued with fear and caution the minds of many leaders in Latin America who had been thinking enviously of the independent, democratic life developing in the United States. Of all these fears the Negro coachman, Toussaint, had become the symbol.

Perhaps under no other circumstances than those of Haiti would he have seemed a great leader. His political and military leadership were simple, almost intuitive. Perhaps his was the wisdom of a primitive mind. But he was suited to the violent times in which he moved and the restless undisciplined forces which he led. One is tempted to believe that if he had been allowed to remain in Haiti much of the subsequent disorder and chaos of that unhappy country could have been avoided. Certainly his brief period of rule had given great promise of peace and orderly development and no other leader could have matched his ascendancy over the minds of the Negro masses.

Yet he himself would have been the first to recognize the uneasy and unstable basis on which his control rested. The liberty of the former slave still found its literal equivalent in the possession of a gun, as Toussaint himself had impressed upon his followers, and this fatal equation, if true, meant that a large price of violence and bloodshed had still to be paid in Haiti. Certainly neither of his immediate successors, neither Christophe nor Dessalines, showed Toussaint's qualities of statesmanship. Neither of them had been the heart and soul of the Negro insurrection as Toussaint had been. Nor did either have his ability in keeping their ambitious, self-seeking lieutenants working together in a common cause. Certainly if anyone could have forged a peaceful future for the Negro republic during the trying years of the early nineteenth century it was he.

He has been called the Black Napoleon. General Laveaux called him "That black Spartacus prophesied by Reynal." But neither term seems entirely appropriate. For he was not like anything which came out of France or out of Rome. Toussaint was American and he was Negro. He was the embodiment of a new force struggling to be born. He was the first great leader of American Negro liberation.

Davis, H. P. Black democracy. New York, Dodge. 1936. p36-86.

James, C. L. R. The Black Jacobins: Toussaint Louverture and the San Domingo revolution. New York, Dial. 1938. 328p.

Mossell, C. W. Toussaint L'Ouverture. Lockport, N.Y. Ward & Cobb. 1896. 484p.

Pauléus Sannon, H. Histoire de Toussaint-Louverture. Port-au-Prince, Imp. Aug. A. Héraux, 1920. Vol. I. 247p.

Rusch, Erwin. Die revolution von Saint Domingue. Hamburg, Friedrichsen, de Gruyter & Co. 1930. 209p.

Stewart, Watt, and Peterson, Harold F. Builders of Latin America. New York and London, Harper. 1942. p 133-45.

Waxman, Percy. The Black Napoleon: the story of Toussaint Louverture New York, Harcourt, Brace. 1931. 298p.

JOSÉ MARÍA MORELOS (1765-1815)

SOLDIER-PRIEST-MARTYR OF MEXICAN INDEPENDENCE

On the island of Janítzio, in Lake Pátzcuaro, not far from his native Morelia, in the state of Michoacán, stands a giant statue of Morelos. To Mexicans and to curious tourists it is a constant reminder of a great man of humble origin who for over four years directed a revolutionary movement which maintained military and political control over the southern provinces of Mexico. One arm raised aloft, with clenched fist, symbolizes the aspiration for liberty. It is a dramatic statue which leaves an indelible impression on the mind. It perpetuates the memory of a priest and a man of the common people, with the blood of Spanish, Negro, and Indian forebears in his veins, who successfully led his poorly armed followers against the larger and better equipped armies of the viceroy, and who almost succeeded in overthrowing the viceregal government and establishing an independent democratic Mexico a decade before independence was in fact achieved. Although his opportunity passed with the end of the Napoleonic wars and the reestablishment of Ferdinand VII in Spain, Morelos left a tradition of successful revolutionary action, and a memory of a social and political program which had far-reaching effects on later Mexican developments. His execution by the Spanish authorities made his name a symbol of Mexico's struggle for independence and democracy, and the statue at Janítzio, in a peculiar fashion, has come to represent all the popular aspirations of the more recent Mexican revolution which began in 1910.

José María Morelos y Pavón was born in Valladolid (present-day Morelia), on September 30, 1765. Son of Manuel Morelos, a carpenter, and of Juana Pavón, daughter of a school teacher, he was registered at the time of his baptism as a legitimate child of Spanish parents. Yet historians have agreed that this registration as Spanish probably concealed the fact, in a way not unusual in those days, that through both parents he was derived from *castas* of mixed Indian and Negro blood. Left an orphan at an early age he was brought up by his uncle. Of his childhood of poverty we have little record. We know that he received a meager education, learning to read and write. Yet his education was certainly very irregular, since, according to his own later account, his boyhood was spent as a shepherd on an hacienda in Apatzingán. Later he worked as a muleteer, driving pack trains between Acapulco, Mexico and Valladolid.

It was not till the age of twenty-five that he entered the Colegio de San Nicolás, in Valladolid, to repair his lack of childhood education and to prepare for the priesthood. The rector of the college was none other than Miguel Hidalgo who was destined soon to become the first leader and martyr of Mexican independence. But there is no evidence of a close relationship between the two at this time. Hidalgo, perhaps, was scarcely aware of this student of mature years destined, presumably, for an obscure Indian parish. Morelos continued his studies in the Tridentine Seminary, and in 1795 journeyed to Mexico City to receive a baccalaureate degree from the University. He had not been a brilliant student, and his training, begun too late in life, like that of many rural priests of the day, was defective. Yet he was far from being simply an ignorant muleteer as he has sometimes been represented in histories. Somehow, in the course of his experience and education, he had become familiar with the liberal revolutionary ideas of the day, and assimilated them so thoroughly that even the shortcomings of his education and culture did not prevent his giving them effective expression at the appropriate time.

His years as a muleteer had also given him a familiarity with the geography of southern Mexico which was later to prove very valuable. From association with the mule drivers, mostly of mixed blood like himself, he had gained an understanding of their aspirations and their ways of life which added greatly to his preparation for leading a popular uprising.

Before receiving the title of presbyter, he lived for a time with his mother and sister in Valladolid, in considerable poverty. Then for two years, from 1796 to 1798, he taught grammar and rhetoric in Uruapan. In the latter year he was assigned to the parish of Churumuco, but soon received a transfer from this parish because the hot climate was having a bad effect upon the health of his mother and sister. The parish of Carácuaro, to which he was then assigned, was the scene of his activities until he joined the revolutionary movement, and it is an interesting commentary on the relation of the Church to the insurrection that he was able to reserve a third of the income of his parish when he joined Hidalgo's forces. He was not an easy master of his flock, for he soon complained to the church authorities that the contributions for his support were not made as due, while his parishioners lodged a complaint with the archbishop against the "severity" of his administration. On the whole, however, he was a faithful and successful priest, and many of his flock followed him into the revolutionary army.

He was short in stature, less than five feet tall, but heavy and robust in appearance. Dark of skin, he had a large face, with broad lips, widely separated, brooding, dark eyes, heavy protruding eyebrows and a large nose, slightly crooked from having been broken against a tree while he was pursuing a bull during his days on the hacienda. His brow was frequently knitted in a frown, and his customary expression was somber, his glance penetrating and fixed. Unmartial in appearance, he usually dressed in clerical garb, although he had a great liking for richly embroidered jackets. A handkerchief was always about his throat, a habit of dress frequently adopted in the southern highlands, presumably for protection against the night cold. On his first campaign he appeared in a Peruvian sombrero, a kind of hat then worn by rich ranchers, a white Moorish cloak which muffled his face, campaign boots, and a pair of pistols. His appearance and dress scarcely commanded respect, and some of Hidalgo's followers apparently made fun of his uncouth looks.

Little is known with certainty about how he first came into contact with the revolutionary movement led by the creole priest Hidalgo. It seems likely, however, that he was in touch with Hidalgo before the latter's uprising in September 1810 and that he had been preparing himself by collecting arms and studying military manuals. There is indeed some evidence of correspondence between the two priests, extending back as far as 1808. Unless he had taken part in the revolutionary planning, it is difficult to explain why Morelos was immediately appointed by Hidalgo to one of the most responsible positions of leadership in the movement.

Miguel Hidalgo, the parish priest of Dolores, was a leader of considerable prestige, a scholar who had conducted the Seminary at Valladolid as we have noted, and a man widely known among the prosperous creoles of Mexico. He made a striking appearance, with his snow white hair and green eyes, and enjoyed the confidence of the numerous members of his class, the creoles, who favored independence and reform in accordance with the prevailing ideas of the French Revolution. Several times he had been in trouble with the Inquisition for his "heretical" views. His uprising represented a widespread conspiracy among the Mexicans who were dissatisfied with the course of events in Spain brought on by Napoleon's effort to impose his brother Joseph as sovereign of that country. The conspiracy was made known to the authorities, however, and Hidalgo was forced to initiate the uprising prematurely. As a result, the support of the creoles was never properly organized. Moreover, his appeal to the suppressed Indians and mestizos, which he symbolized by using the banner of the Virgin of Guadalupe, the patron saint of the Indians, soon gave his whole movement the character of a turbulent, uncontrolled social uprising, which turned many of the more cautious creoles against him.

He swept across central Mexico during the late months of 1810 and early 1811, a kind of demiurge, stirring the long subject masses to an amorphous rebellion which only the great force of his personality could in any measure control. He quickly dominated all of the central plateau, so that he probably could have captured the largely defenseless city of Mexico with ease. Why he did not do so has always been a matter of speculation, but there is some reason for thinking that he was afraid to turn his almost unmanageable horde loose on this center of European culture.

The first meeting of the two leaders occurred in October 1810, at the little town of Charo, just after Hidalgo's capture of Valladolid. Hidalgo was at the point of beginning that movement toward the north which was to end disastrously a few months later, and he entrusted Morelos with the task of raising an army in the south, with the ultimate objective of capturing the Pacific port of Acapulco.

There has been much difference among writers over Morelos' ability as a military leader, although recent Mexican historians incline toward recognizing in him a genius for strategy and tactics, as well as qualities of moral leadership. His first campaign, during 1810 and 1811, was directed chiefly toward securing arms, raising and organizing an army in the south, and, as already noted, capturing Acapulco if possible. It was during the months of this campaign that Hidalgo was captured and executed. But Hidalgo's defeat in no way lessened Morelos' activity, which continued to be an almost unbroken chain of successes.

The scene of the rebellion now shifted, under Morelos, to the southern provinces. He was particularly successful in gaining the support of the Galeana brothers, and of the Bravo brothers, rich landowners, who raised personal forces and became his principal lieutenants during the succeeding years. His principal objectives, securing arms and raising an army, were soon fulfilled, and he was able to put an army of eight thousand men into the field. Stores of arms were captured, and his forces were swollen with contingents of Negroes and Indians, as well as with the militia of the region. Acapulco was not captured, but was cut off from the rest of the region. One of his principal objectives was to prevent mobilization of the militia and in this he was strikingly successful, much of the militia actually joining his army. The viceroy thus had to divert forces from other areas into the south.

His most striking victory over the royalists in this campaign was at Chichihualco, where the cavalry of the Bravo brothers and the Negro troops of the Galeana brothers gave a good account of themselves. This success opened the way for the occupation of Chilpancingo. Tixtla and Chilapa were also captured and the first campaign ended in August 1811 with a well organized insurgent army in control of much of the present state of Guerrero. It was an army which had shown it could hold its own in the field against superior royalist forces, and which was acting in cooperation with insurgent forces elsewhere in the country.

Morelos' second campaign opened in November 1811, and included a striking victory over royalist forces at Izúcar, the occupation of Cuauhtla and Taxco, and the capture by storm of Tenancingo. After the victory at Izúcar he passed up the opportunity to march on Puebla and after Tenancingo he failed to take advantage of a similar opportunity to pursue the defeated royalist forces to Toluca. Yet this second campaign was a striking success, on the whole, and the forces of independence were at the height of their power at the end of 1811. With his little army of 8000 Morelos held at bay royalist forces of about 86,000 men. The city of Mexico was in grave danger, threatened from three sides, the viceroy wrote to General Calleja, who was then besieging Morelos in Cuauhtla. Yet in spite of the many victories he had gained, Morelos was unable to take the offensive against the more numerous and better equipped royalist forces. He led a heroic seventy-two-day defense of Cuauhtla, and brought this second campaign to an end on May 2, 1812, when he and his forces escaped from the city to begin again the painful task of building up and equipping a strong armed force.

His third campaign, from June to November 1812, centered again in the Guerrero region, although for a brief time he occupied Orizaba as the result of operations centering in Tehuacán, operations which threatened the main communications of Mexico City with the port of Vera Cruz and with Puebla. He also occupied Oaxaca, while his lieutenant, Guerrero, conducted a successful campaign on the Isthmus of Tehuantepec. Then in January 1813 he marched on Acapulco, and after a long siege, reduced this last remaining royalist stronghold in the south.

The months from August to November 1813 were taken up principally with the meeting of a congress at Chilpancingo, and with plans for the political organization of the country. Morelos' principal purpose in calling the Congress was to give the movement a broader political basis than the unsatisfactory junta or committee inherited from the days of Hidalgo, which had lost prestige through its inability to reconcile differences of the rival leaders, or exert effective leadership itself. Morelos had now been, for some time, the principal chieftain of the independence movement. The Congress was his plan and under his leadership it became the legal government of the very extensive areas in the south of Mexico occupied by the insurgents. Congress soon declared Mexican independence from Spain, giving up the mask of loyalty to the deposed Ferdinand VII which Hidalgo had assumed in 1810. It proclaimed the abolition of slavery, of castes and special privileges, and of the payment of tribute; it also proclaimed popular sovereignty and limited officeholding to Americans. Morelos was named Generalissimo and entrusted with the executive power. The Congress went on to draw up a democratic constitution which was proclaimed the following year.

The siege of Acapulco and the meeting of the Congress gave the new viceroy, Calleja, time to develop plans for suppressing the rebellion by attacking, one by one, the rebel bands which were separated from Morelos, while preparing a strong force to await the latter in whatever direction he might move. Morelos was determined, however, to remain on the offensive and made plans to capture Valladolid. He was nearly successful in carrying it by storm, but failed at the last moment. This failure was the fatal turning point in his military career. Royal reinforcements arrived before the capture was complete and turned what had been an insurgent victory into a disastrous defeat. In this encounter it was Colonel Augustín Iturbide (later Emperor) who, in a daring and surprise cavalry attack, delivered the decisive blow. Another defeat at Puruarán left Morelos with greatly reduced forces, and in a perilous military situation. Meanwhile Oaxaca and Acapulco were recovered by the forces of the viceroy.

The Congress and Morelos then determined on a drastic move—to transfer the seat of government to Tehuacán, scene of some of Morelos' most brilliant exploits in an earlier period. It involved a dangerous march through territory held by enemy troops, mountainous terrain where an ambush was possible at any turn. Yet his little force of one thousand men (only five hundred had firearms), guarding the members of Congress, almost succeeded in this seemingly impossible undertaking. Winding their way along the Mezcala River, they misled their pursuers and almost escaped them. At last they were forced to accept battle—the fatal defeat of Tezmalaca. Seeing that victory was impossible, Morelos gave orders for each man to save himself. Attempting to escape alone, without a bodyguard, he was soon captured.

He had acquired a reputation for cruelty because of the execution of royalist leaders. However, in the light of the fact that all rebel leaders faced the same fate, if captured, these executions are hardly to be attributed to wanton cruelty, but rather to policy. They were drastic, perhaps, but no more drastic than the policy of the Spanish authorities. After his capture he was brought to the royalist commanders, Concha and Villasana. The latter asked him: "What would you do if the situation were reversed and you had captured me or Señor Concha?"

"I should give you two hours to make your confession and then I would shoot you," was the laconic reply.

But Morelos was not dealt with so mercifully. He was not executed immediately, but was sent to Mexico City, where he was lodged in the prison of the Inquisition, his ultimate sentence to death a foregone conclusion. Hidalgo and other revolutionary leaders previously captured had met that fate. But the government wished to make as great an impression as possible in this case, and to give his trial and execution the maximum notoriety for its effect on public opinion. The Inquisition, revived for the purpose, found him guilty of heresy and subjected him to an auto-da-fé in which he was publicly divested of clerical authority, then turned over to the secular authorities. He was now condemned to death, and, after some little delay, executed by a firing squad at the little village of San Cristobal Ecatepec on December 22, 1815.

His capture and execution brought to a tragic end the first phase of the Mexican movement for independence. As Alfonso Teja Zabre has pointed out in a recent biography,[1] Morelos had become "the soul of the war and the personification of the cause of independence" to the extent that his capture was the equivalent of a great decisive battle. For the next six years the cause of independence was to be kept alive only by desperate isolated guerrilla bands.

Morelos may or may not have been a great military strategist and tactician, although his career shows at least some indications of military genius. Serious criticisms have been made against his conduct of the attack on Valladolid, and, as noted, he has been charged with failing to take full advantage of some of his earlier victories. These shortcomings are balanced by his brilliant campaigns centering in Tehuacán, the occupation of Orizaba and Oaxaca, and the brave defense of Cuauhtla. Of his moral and political leadership there is little doubt. He, alone, among the early leaders of Mexican independence was able to build a cohesive, organized force out of the ragged and poorly equipped guerrilla bands of rival leaders, and to give them a plan of campaign.

Like Washington, he was often greatest in defeat. Moreover, it was he who showed the clearest political sense among these early leaders. When Ignacio Rayón, president of the revolutionary junta established following the capture of Hidalgo, proposed a constitution in 1812, Morelos opposed it because it maintained the fiction of loyalty to King Ferdinand. A year later he assembled a national congress at Chilpancingo and led it in abolishing this fiction by a declaration of independence. More than any other member of the congress he was responsible for its revolutionary action abolishing the privileges of race and caste and guaranteeing liberty to all "Americans." Yet his sense of the political realities led him to oppose the constitution upon which the congress agreed, contrary to his recommendations, because it vested supreme power in a congress and created a weak triumvirate executive.

The defeat of Napoleon in Spain and the proclamation of Ferdinand VII as king in 1813 had much to do with the sudden collapse of the Morelos movement. Not only were the loyalists greatly strengthened in their determination to resist, but friends of the revolutionary cause were temporarily discouraged by the turn of events and by the vanishing of any prospect of outside military assistance. Yet Morelos had shown that this popular uprising could be given form and direction. He had conquered and gov-

[1] Teja Zabre, Alfonso. *Morelos.* Buenos Aires and Mexico, Espasa-Calpe. 1946. 171p.

erned a considerable part of Mexico, and had given the revolutionary movement a democratic program, including the abolition of slavery, social castes, and privileges. But for the turn of events in Europe, his leadership might have brought independence to Mexico in 1813 or 1814 rather than seven years later.

His instructions to the revolutionary chieftains included the confiscation of the wealth of Spanish landowners and mineowners, and the division of their wealth among the poor of the vicinity after the needs of the army had been supplied. In part this was a measure of war, but the intent was clearly to bring about a redistribution of wealth. Americans who owed debts to Spaniards were not obliged to pay them, he declared, but Spaniards were to pay all debts owed to Americans. The *alcabala* or sales tax was abolished, and in its place import taxes and a 5 per cent income tax were proclaimed. Morelos consistently stated that he was not a rebel against the Mexican government nor against the Church, but that he was leading an American revolution against Europeans and European influences. His political concepts and program forecast much of what the Mexican nation was to struggle to achieve through years of bitter civil strife during the half century following his death.

Lansing, M. F. Liberators and heroes of Mexico and Central America. New York, Page. 1941. 299p. "Morelos of Mexico." p39-55.

Magner, James A. Men of Mexico. Milwaukee, Bruce Publishing Company. 1942. 614p. Ch. IX, "José María Morelos."

Sierra, Justo. Evolución política del pueblo Mexicano. México, Fondo de Cultura Económica. 1940. 480p. p 169-175 and *passim*.

Teja Zabre, Alfonso. Morelos. Buenos Aires, Colección Austral. 1946. 211p. (An earlier biography by the same author was published in Madrid in 1934.)

MARIANO MORENO (1778-1811)

THE MAN OF MAY

The May Revolution (1810) in Buenos Aires not only constituted the most decisive turn in the chain of events resulting in Argentine independence, but exercised a profound influence over the whole movement for independence in Spanish America. The outstanding figure during the critical months which followed was Mariano Moreno, secretary of the revolutionary junta. Leader of a small determined liberal faction in the city, for a brief period he showed the power of leadership based on political-economic objectives clearly conceived and applied practically with determination and confidence as well as clear understanding of the psychological, political, and economic factors involved. "No one in so little time did more," wrote the Argentine Alberto Ghiraldes.

Moreno's political career provides an excellent example of the powerful effect, in time of crisis, of a combination of a revolutionary press and determined political leadership. He is an example of the man who is distinguished both for leadership in ideas and in action. In this respect his career suggests the brilliant and tragic course of Marat, although his devotion to moral concepts is more reminiscent of Robespierre, while his ringing phraseology, generalized in Jacobin language, suggests an analogy to Jefferson. At all events his facile pen, deriving its authority in part from its expression of the economic aspirations of Buenos Aires, and in part from its apt phrasing of universal principles and rights, gave fundamental direction and shape to Argentina's early independent course, and, indirectly, to the movement throughout Spanish South America.

In spite of his frail physique—perhaps partly because of it—his physical appearance attracted attention in any gathering of which he was a part. A high, broad forehead, a straight, somewhat large nose, heavy black hair, and thin, tight lips served to emphasize his deep-set eyes, which, according to his contemporaries, seemed constantly fixed in a melancholy gaze on some distant horizon. It was a face strongly suggestive of Beethoven or Victor Hugo, and the physical fascination which he exercised went far to explain his great mastery over men.

Mariano Moreno was born in Buenos Aires on September 23, 1778. His father, Manuel, descended from a poor but noble Spanish family, had come to America as secretary to the governor of Havana. Subsequently he had held a number of official posts under the viceregal government in Buenos Aires. His mother, Ana María Valle, the daughter of a former

royal treasurer, was a woman of profound spiritual character who exercised
great influence over her son's life. In eighteenth century Buenos Aires,
where few women could read and write, she was exceptional for her excellent educational attainments.

It was she who initiated his education, teaching him to read and write.
He then attended the Escuela del Rey, and at twelve entered the Colegio de
San Carlos, a secondary school established by the City of Buenos Aires in
1783, which offered a program more secular and less theological than was
customary in schools of its type. Here he studied Latin grammar, philosophy, and theology, and, what was more important, came under the influence
of a Franciscan, Cayetano Rodríguez, an avid student of the literature of the
Enlightenment, who gave him access to the library of his monastery. By the
age of twenty Moreno had developed into a young man of serious intellectual interests, active in spite of somewhat delicate health, fiery in temperament, and of great sensibility. There was no university in Buenos Aires,
and the expense of the long journey to the University of Chuquisaca in Peru
was beyond the means of his family, so that continuation of his education
seemed difficult if not impossible.

Yet, as happens so often, where there is a strong will, a way is found.
A fortunate increase in his father's salary and the assistance of a rich priest
of the Archbishopric of Chuquisaca enabled him to set out on the long two
and a half month's journey overland to Chuquisaca in 1799. The new intellectual eagerness which had begun to penetrate Spanish America in the
last decades of the eighteenth century found one of its most important centers in this old university of Upper Peru, and Moreno, as a student, was to
play an active role in the activities which made it the intellectual center of
the independence movement. A letter of introduction to Canon Terrazas
brought him at once into an intellectual group devoted to the principle of
the free examination of all ideas. The Caroline Academy, the school within
the University in which he enrolled, was devoted to the study of Roman and
Indian law, but it was also an active center of these new ideas.

Memories of the Indian uprisings led by Tupac Amarú and Tupac
Katari were still fresh in Upper Peru, and Victorian de Villava's study of
the *mita* in Potosí stirred Moreno's sympathy for the oppressed Indian pop-
ulations. This interest in the oppressed Indian appeared in his thesis, presented for his degree in 1802, in which he made a brilliant exposition of the
violence done to the Spanish laws which were intended to protect the Indian.
Reading the *Política indiana* of Solórzano Pereira likewise brought home to
him the political and economic handicaps under which the creoles lived. In
the library of Canon Terrazas he studied the works of the French revolutionary philosophers. The *Histoire philosophique et politique des établissements
et du commerce des Européens dans les deux Indes* of the Abbé Raynal,

which he read at this time, exercised a great formative influence on his mind. Raynal predicted a revolution in Spanish America led by the creoles, in which freedom of conscience and freedom of trade would be joined with the encouragement of agriculture, the kind of revolution in which Moreno himself was to take part.

Returning to Buenos Aires in 1805, he brought with him a young bride, María Guadalupe Cuenca, and a child born early that year. The path to success was a difficult one for a creole lawyer under the Spanish colonial system, so that the quickness with which he won the confidence of a wealthy and powerful clientele was a striking recognition of his talents. He became, almost at once, a man of mark in the viceregal capital.

Then, in 1806, came a series of events which profoundly altered the course of this professional career. The British occupied Buenos Aires in that year. The viceroy fled and, almost immediately, a popular uprising drove out the invader and, later, defeated a second British expedition. The uprising was led by Santiago de Liniers, a French army officer, who had retired after service in the Spanish army. Keenly moved, Moreno made extensive notes of the public reaction, talked with innumerable witnesses, and wrote his *Memorias* on the occupation, the only thing he ever wrote without a political purpose. In the meeting of the *cabildo*, or municipal council, called by Liniers to depose the viceroy, and in the open meeting of the *cabildo* on January 1, 1809, he emerged as an effective spokesman of the creoles of Buenos Aires who were ready to support an independent course of action in Argentina while professing loyalty to the deposed King Ferdinand VII.

Manuel Belgrano, one of the earliest advocates of independence, had urged Liniers, who was then acting as viceroy, to open the port of Buenos Aires to world commerce. But it was Moreno who gave this proposal its classic form and moving force in his *Representación . . . de los hacendados . . .* (Memorial of the Landowners) prepared at the request of the new Spanish viceroy Cisneros, who replaced Liniers. His argument based on "the imperious law of necessity, . . . before which all other laws yield" was phrased in simple and cogent terms, answering the arguments of the monopolists and urging freedom of commerce for two years. Translated into Portuguese by José da Silva Lisboa after Moreno's death, this essay was to play an almost equally important role in shaping the movement for free trade in Brazil, a movement which, under the guidance of José Bonifacio de Andrada paved the way for Brazilian independence. Moreno had formulated the economic aspirations of Buenos Aires in terms of the liberal economic and political principles. For the next two years he became increasingly the spokesman and representative of these aspirations in the series of rapid political changes by which Buenos Aires undertook to organize the affairs of the viceroyalty in accordance with liberal principles—a tendency which was the source of so much of the subsequent Argentine political difficulty. Realizing the potential influence of the essay as a revolutionary document, the viceroy, Cisneros, forbade its publication. But manuscript copies circulated freely, and in Rio de Janeiro and London the work came into the hands of the English, who hailed it with great approval.

Moreno soon became the leading spokesman of a group of young radicals who met by custom in the Café de Marcos, across from the Church of San Ignacio. It was a group of young republicans who were frequently impatient with the older and more cautious Belgrano, who felt that a monarchy under a Bourbon prince would be a more suitable government for the new nation if it became independent. They differed also with the ideas of Liniers, who preferred orienting Argentine policy in the direction of closer cooperation with Napoleonic France. But factionalism had not yet developed among the revolutionary leaders to the point which it was to reach a few years later. Now the principal influence of the Café de Marcos group was directed to enlisting the support of the others in a move to replace the viceroy with a governmental junta. This they were successful in doing when news arrived from Spain that Napoleon had captured Gerona and established his mastery over the mother country.

In 1808 Napoleon had deposed the weak Spanish king, Carlos IV, and forced his son Ferdinand to renounce the crown, installing his own brother Joseph in their place. But Napoleon had underestimated the resistance of the Spanish people, and his invasion of Spain was the beginning of a long struggle which eventually helped to bring about his downfall. A revolutionary junta was formed at Seville to lead the Spanish resistance, and soon a regency was established in the name of Ferdinand. At first the Spanish Americans rallied to the cause of the junta. They refused to receive the agents of Napoleon and some of them sent delegates to the Cortes which was called by the regency. But the difficulties of the Spanish monarchy also worked to encourage many groups in America in whom the idea of independence was already taking form. This was the tendency which Moreno and his friends represented, and Napoleon's apparent victory in 1810 seemed to be just the signal for which they had been waiting, since the cause of Ferdinand seemed to be doomed.

An exciting series of open meetings of the Buenos Aires *cabildo* was held from May 22 to May 25, 1810. These meetings the Argentines call their May revolution, and the outcome was what the radicals wanted: the appointment of a revolutionary junta to replace the viceroy, Cisneros. The turning point came when Cornelio Saavedra, commander of the militia regiment of nobles, told the viceroy that he could no longer count on the loyalty of his troops. Saavedra became president of the junta, and Moreno, who, needless to say, had taken an active part in the proceedings, was named secretary for government and war. He quickly became the guiding spirit and intelligence of the junta. Although he was only a secretary and not a member of the executive junta, conservative opposition in the provinces and the plotting of royalist leaders in the capital soon produced a crisis which gave him the opportunity to assume almost the powers of a dictator. His determined will forced the outfitting of military expeditions to command the loyalty of the provinces, and to meet the threat of armed invasion from Peru.

With Belgrano he started to publish the *Gaceta de Buenos Aires*. Belgrano soon left for the interior with the army, but Moreno made of this semiweekly journal a highly effective instrument for the expression of his views and plans. One of the most frequent contributors to the *Gaceta* was the brilliant mulatto, Bernardo Monteagudo, who later formulated Bolívar's plan for a Pan American Congress.[1] Other important measures at this time removed the last obstacles to freedom of commerce and lifted the restrictions on the mining of precious metals. By gaining the confidence of the British representative in Rio de Janeiro, Lord Strangford, Moreno succeeded in lifting the blockade of Buenos Aires. He prevailed upon Lord Strangford to inform the British government that unless protection were offered to the junta the latter would declare the independence of Argentina prematurely under French guaranty. In June he directed the move which led to the arrest and exile of the ex-viceroy Cisneros and the members of the *audiencia*. He urged and secured approval by the junta of severe measures for dealing with leaders of the first movement of open opposition, centering in Córdoba.

The junta, under his direction, annulled the rule requiring foreigners to consign goods through a registered merchant. Vigorous measures were also taken to suppress contraband trade. Usury was restricted, and an attempt was made to regulate the slaughter of cattle and sheep, an industry which was already becoming important in relation to international trade. The ports of Maldonado, Rio Negro, and Ensenada were opened to seagoing commerce. The cavalry branch of the army was reorganized and a gun manufactory established. The new government founded a public library and a school of mathematics, constructed new elementary school buildings and a new building for an academy of music, and increased the salaries of teachers.

Moreno's manifesto of October 9, 1810, following the execution of the Córdoba conspirators, is one of his outstanding political documents. Although repeating professions of loyalty to Ferdinand, the manifesto breathes the doctrine of popular sovereignty in every paragraph. It is "the people from whom the Kings derive all the power with which they govern." The conspirators had been guilty of more than treason, he wrote. "As mag-

[1] See Harold E. Davis, *Makers of Democracy in Latin America.* p35-8.

istrates their crime was the more enormous and sacrilegious violation of the faith which they owe to the public confidence and to the constitutional laws of their offices."

Up to the eve of the assembly of Congress, called for late in 1810, the record of the junta under Moreno's direction was one of striking successes gained against tremendous odds by the militant minority which he represented. The full extent and tenor of his revolutionary ideas and plans appeared in an article in the *Gaceta* for November 6 of that year. The new congress, he wrote, should act the role of the French Estates General. It should adopt a constitution for the nascent nation to ensure the institutions of the future. A new code of laws should "establish honesty of customs, security of persons, protection of their rights, the duties of officials, the obligations of the subject, and the limits of obedience." In the spirit of Rousseau, he called for exercise of the *general will* in establishing a democracy based upon individual liberty and the moral elevation of individuals. His previous reticence on the question of independence was now gone almost completely as he stated his proposals for a revolutionary constitution. Since government in America was based upon conquest, there was no social compact which needed to be considered in the establishment of a government. This new government would be independent in fact, although loyal to Ferdinand. Considering the question of federating all the American provinces of the Spanish empire, he concluded that it was impractical, for reasons largely geographical. Each one of the provinces, he said, would have to decide its own destiny.

Moreno had not hesitated to use force to suppress counterrevolution, and the severity of his measures against the Córdoba leaders as well as against officials everywhere who failed to support the revolutionary movements soon gave rise to serious criticism. He was charged with tyranny, cruelty, and unscrupulousness. His reputed willingness to resort to plot, intrigue, and conspiracy to attain his ends made him suspect. Opposition was particularly strong among moderate and conservative leaders in the provinces, who not only were disturbed at the rapid march of events but were coming to feel, also, that Moreno and his progressive young creole supporters represented too largely the economic and political interests of the capital only. Nor could they count on the united support of all the revolutionary forces of the capital, for factionalism had appeared in the ranks of the junta. Cornelio Saavedra, the president, and a moderate, was increasingly disturbed at some of Moreno's measures and at his driving leadership. Increasingly the revolutionary leaders were known as *Morenistas* or *Saavedristas,* and the rift between the two groups was widening. It was to become fatal to Moreno when Saavedra later threw in his lot with the provincial leaders when they assembled for the congress.

That Moreno realized the precariousness of his political and personal position, as the members of the newly summoned Congress began to assemble, appears from his writings in the *Gaceta* during the month of October. Threats were made against him. But he continued to go unguarded on the streets, running the risk of assassination, and waited for his opponents to show themselves openly. Meanwhile he took a further radical step in the decree of December 3, 1810, by which the junta ordered that future official appointments should be given only to native-born Argentines. Europeans were urged to establish themselves permanently in the country, and to engage in agriculture and other economic activities. Another egalitarian decree of December 6 suppressed the old ceremonial honors which had been accorded the President of the Junta, and gave further offense to those who felt Moreno was moving too rapidly in the direction of republicanism. This decree wounded Saavedra particularly and brought out into the open a growing conflict between the tendencies and parties which the two men represented. It is a conflict which has been aptly characterized by the Argentine historian, Ricardo Levene, as the first open clash between two historical forces, "turbulent democracy," which requires strong central government, and "federal democracy."

Joel R. Poinsett, the first agent of the United States to Buenos Aires, wrote two years later (1813) that Moreno "was the principal Engine of the revolution and the founder of everything useful since. He fell a sacrifice to the violence of his own passions and to the animosity of Saavedra." By December 1810 the forces which were to bring this overthrow had appeared. Provincial conservative opposition led by Dean Gregorio Funes of Córdoba and the moderates who centered around Saavedra found their opportunity later in December, after news of the success of the military expeditions in the interior relieved the feeling of political crisis. On December 18, over Moreno's opposition, the provincial deputies present in Buenos Aires attended a meeting of the junta and voted to incorporate themselves in that body. Moreno then announced his resignation, which the junta at first refused to accept. But this proved to be his final elimination from power, for he refused to resume his post, although accepting a diplomatic mission to Rio de Janeiro and London. The mission to Brazil and Britain was in effect a form of exile, or at least so Lord Strangford wrote to Wellesley. Meanwhile he had managed to avoid involvement in an abortive uprising of his friends early in January 1811.

He sailed for London on January 24, aboard the *Farna,* saying to his friends, as he left, "I go, but the tail which I leave is very long." [2] His journey was never completed, for he died aboard ship on March 8, 1811.

The tail which he left behind was indeed a long one, reaching far into Argentine political life and history. The triumph of his enemies was brief.

---

[2] *"Yo me voy, pero la cola que dejo es muy larga."*

As a result of his rule, Argentina had been committeed irrevocably to the course of revolution. Although a formal declaration of independence was to wait five more years, there was never any question after 1811 that the Argentine course lay in that direction. The Café de Marcos remained a center for the meeting and plotting of his friends, and they eventually contributed to the uprising of September 1811 and the establishment of the Triumvirate which brought in Moreno's spiritual successor, Bernardino Rivadavia.

Moreno's life was short, and his public career a brief seven months. He was not yet thirty-three at the time of his death, yet he had left his stamp on Argentine life and politics. The secret of his meteoric rise and fall seems to have been that where others hesitated or vacillated, he moved as by a sure instinct to accept those measures best adapted to secure the objectives of the revolutionary group of creoles in Buenos Aires who were the nucleus of the independence movement. Swiftly and surely his leadership was taking Argentina in the direction of independence and a democratic constitution based upon the liberal political and economic philosophy of his day, when his career was cut short. He is rightly famed as the Man of the May, the outstanding figure in the May Revolution, "the principal Engine of the revolution." But he was also the first of a series of great liberal leaders in Argentina, and he stands at the forefront of the strong liberal tradition in her history.

Bagú, Sergio. Mariano Moreno. Buenos Aires, Claridad. 1939. 284p.

Elordi, Guillermo F. Mariano Moreno, ciudadano ilustre. Buenos Aires, La Facultad. 1938. 275p.

Ghiraldo, Alberto. Libertadores de América. Santiago de Chile, Ercilla. 1935. p61-2.

Gondra, Luis Roque, and others. El pensamiento económico latino-americano. México, Fondo de Cultura Económica. 1945. p 18, 76

Hispanic American Historical Review. 14:450-76. May 1934. Mariano Moreno: the making of an insurgent. Harold F. Peterson.

Levene, Ricardo. Ensayo histórico sobre la revolución de mayo y Mariano Moreno. (Contribución al estudio de los aspectos político, jurídico y económico de la revolución de 1810) Buenos Aires, Facultad de Derecho y Ciencias Sociales. 1920-21. 2v. Especially v 1.

Levene, Ricardo. A history of Argentina. (Tr. and ed. by William Spence Robertson) (Inter-American historical series, v 1) Chapel Hill, University of North Carolina Press. 1937. 565p. Especially ch. 25-29.

Levene, Ricardo, ed. Pensamiento vivo de Mariano Moreno. Buenos Aires, Losada. 1942. 235p.

Stewart, Watt, and Peterson, Harold F. Builders of Latin America. New York and London, Harper. 1942. p 106-16.

BERNARDINO RIVADAVIA (1780-1845)

ILL-STARRED FIRST PRESIDENT OF ARGENTINA

The name of Bernardino Rivadavia is so closely identified with the years from 1811 to 1826 in the early history of Argentina that the period is usually referred to as the epoch of Rivadavia. Evey aspect of the nascent nation's development felt the imprint of his mind and personality. Moreover, he is a striking example of the political leader who, though rising from comparative obscurity, seems to have been prepared by nature or Providence to meet the exigencies of the occasion. Yet his efforts were constantly thwarted and defeated by persistent personal and political misfortune.

In general he resumed the revolutionary republican tendencies inaugurated by Mariano Moreno, working for the establishment of an independent republic in days when constitutional monarchy was the preference of most of the influential Argentine leaders. He was the first president of a constitutional republic in Argentina. Yet his tendency toward moderation was so strong and his political flexibility so great in seeking practical political policies and measures, that for several years, between the first and second periods of his political action in Argentina, he represented his country in Europe in the search for a prince to act as constitutional monarch. Though his sympathies were with the ardent Bernardo Monteagudo, Rivadavia recoiled from the latter's radical agitation and willingness to urge extreme measures, even dictatorship, and he suppressed the officially supported *Gaceta de Buenos Aires* when Monteagudo began to use it for the violent expression of his views. In the complicated struggle for leadership of the independence movement between Buenos Aires and the provinces, which later became the conflict of unitarism and federalism, Rivadavia was the voice of Buenos Aires and unitarism. From this identification with the interests of the metropolis came much of his political strength as well as many of his mistakes.

He was born on May 20, 1780 in Buenos Aires. His father, Benito González Rivadavia, was a wealthy lawyer who held important posts in the government in Buenos Aires. His mother, Josefa Rivadavia, a cousin of her husband, likewise came from an important family of the viceregal city. It was an austere household in which Bernardino grew up, austere to the point that he never knew the normal play of a child. His mother died when he was six or seven and a stepmother took her place. She was kind to the boy, but brought on a violent quarrel between his two older sisters and his father which thereafter colored the family life with feelings of intense passion and hatred. Bernardino's first teacher was a priest, Marcos Salcedo. In the Colegio Real de San Carlos of Buenos Aires, he afterwards studied grammar, philosophy, and theology, and came into contact with the new revolutionary ideas of the day. As a student he was intensely serious and fanatically religious.

At the age of twenty-three, without having completed a professional course in either theology or law, he began to assume an active part in his father's many enterprises and to embark on some of his own. A few years later he was attacked by Mariano Moreno for engaging in legal work without a title, but apparently he had prepared himself by work with his father. Most of his business enterprises were in partnership with his father, and appear to have been uniformly unsuccessful. The most striking instance was the purchase at public sale of the ship *Juan Federico,* which was reclaimed in the name of a former owner just as expensive repairs were completed. Eventually he regained possession, only to have his vessel destroyed by a severe storm while standing in harbor. Another effort to separate himself from an unsuccessful business partnership brought a clash with young Mariano Moreno, who was engaged as lawyer by the disgruntled partner, and marked the first appearance of a jealous rivalry between these two young men who were destined to play such prominent and closely related roles in the May Revolution and its subsequent developments.

Rivadavia and his father both took an active part in the defense of Buenos Aires against the second British invasion in 1807. Bernardino commanded a company of militia in the defense and was promised a grant of public lands by Liniers for his services. This was the occasion of another disappointment, for he never received the land. He was disappointed, also, when Liniers failed to carry out his promise to appoint him *alférez real* (royal standard-bearer), a petty office, but one of considerable prestige in Buenos Aires. Just at this time news arrived that Ferdinand and Carlos had been deposed by Napoleon, and Liniers was forced to withdraw the nomination of his protégé because of the political agitation which Mariano Moreno and his friends were carrying on in the city. Needless to say, the *Morenistas* were not slow in making political capital of this frustration of petty ambition and vanity, and Bernardino was immediately dubbed "alférez for a day" by the wits of the city.

In 1809 he married Juanita del Pino y Vera, daughter of a former viceroy. Juanita was a charming, loyal, and sympathetic wife, who by her understanding and intelligence contributed greatly to Bernardino's success. But his marriage into this royalist, viceregal family made him the subject of bitter criticism by both friends and enemies. It was particularly embarrassing to have in his own house a brother-in-law who was known openly as a royalist and who was later to command a royalist fleet which bombarded

Buenos Aires. But Bernardino's sense of family loyalty and responsibility was too great to permit these political differences to bring a break in family ties.

What kind of person was this young man, now approaching thirty years of age? His stocky, short stature seemed little suited to dominate men. Yet he had learned that he could command men in the defense of Buenos Aires. The deficiency of his stature was compensated for by a dominating attitude and facial expression. A high receding forehead, curly black hair, heavy eyebrows, large protruding black eyes which flashed with a steely brilliance, high, dark cheeks, a long straight nose surmounting heavy lips and a stubborn chin—his features in general were ugly, but it was a striking ugliness, which, with his habitual expression of disdain made him a man to be marked in an assembly. A succession of failures in business and personal affairs had brought disillusionment, and he had learned to receive calumny by cloaking himself in a mantle of contemptuous indifference. Although his business failures had revealed an overly adventurous and optimistic spirit, they had also shown a stubborn determination, a quality he shared with his father, for neither had ever given up a quarrel or a law suit resulting from his affairs, but had always fought through to the bitter end. In marked contrast with the fiery, animated Mariano Moreno, whose place he was later to assume, he was cold, reserved and serious in speech, always courteous, cultivating the manner of an aristocrat, a manner to which the prestige of his family connections and social position readily lent themselves. Just how he had come under the influence of Manuel Belgrano is not clear, but like many young men of the city, he had been greatly influenced by Belgrano's revolutionary ideas, and had formed a friendship with him which was to be lifelong.

Rivadavia's participation in the open meeting of the *cabildo* on May 25, 1810, which deposed the Spanish viceroy Cisneros and began the movement for independence, was a decided break with all the traditions of the families of his father, his mother, and his wife. Characteristically he was silent throughout the proceedings, but when he came to cast his vote, he did so in the exact language of Moreno. He took no active part in the government under the first junta, which was ruled by Moreno's genius. A few months after the latter's resignation and departure for England, Rivadavia, too, was exiled to a fortress near the Indian frontier when the bombardment of the port by a Spanish fleet under the command of his brother-in-law, Michelena, gave the Committee on Security an occasion to strike at him for his attacks on the government. While in exile, however, he was chosen by the electors of Buenos Aires as one of the *consultores del gobierno*. Returning to Buenos Aires, he was soon named secretary to the triumvirate established in September 1811.

The junta, which contained representatives of the provinces, had been constituted as a legislative body when the triumvirate was established, but its powers were not defined. It soon attempted to assert authority over the triumvirate. Rivadavia met this threat by turning for support to the *cabildo,* the city council which had played such a prominent role in the May Revolution of 1810. The *cabildo's* position in the government was anamolous, since it represented simply the province of Buenos Aires, in the absence of any other effective provincial government. Yet, since 1807, it had in a number of occasions acted as the government of the viceroyalty. The triumvirate now issued a statute which limited the powers of the junta, and when this action threatened to result in an armed uprising, dissolved the junta and called for the election of a national assembly. Unfortunately, by thus identifying the leadership of the revolution with the *cabildo* and with the province of Buenos Aires, Rivadavia stimulated the already apparent jealousy and rivalry between Buenos Aires and the other provinces. When the assembly which succeeded the junta undertook again to assert control over the triumvirate, this time by blocking Rivadavia's election as interim triumvir, he dissolved the assembly again (April 1812), intensifying the conflict further.

During the few feverish months in which he exercised control as minister, he initiated a number of reforms, foreshadowing those of the next decade. He created a general staff and reorganized the army, granted amnesty to political prisoners and exiles, reduced salaries and pensions, established personal guaranties, including freedom of the press, appointed a junta to guard this freedom of expression, announced the emancipation of Negro slaves, established the National Library projected by Moreno, and established many schools. A royalist conspiracy led by Alzaga was discovered and suppressed by Rivadavia's vigilance, almost single handedly, because the triumvirs refused at first to take it seriously. When the tide of popular fury turned against all Spaniards in a wave of denunciations, it was his firm stand which called a halt. However costly it might be in public favor, this stubborn young man was seldom moved from what he felt to be his duty. Faced with the double threat of a royalist invasion from Upper Peru and a Portuguese army in Uruguay, he made a truce with the Spanish viceroy, Elío, in Montevideo, on condition of the immediate withdrawal of the Portuguese troops. When the agreement was not carried out, he organized and dispatched troops to the Uruguayan frontier. This energetic action brought the exertion of British influence and another truce.

Although his every instinct led him to avoid identification with any party, the attacks of such radical *Morenistas* as Bernardo Monteagudo forced him at last to a closer union with the moderate party of Saavedra. The opportunity of his opponents came when the new national assembly, late in 1812, elected two *Saavedrista* triumvirs to serve with Pueyrredón. Belgrano's unexpected victory over the royalists at Tucumán, in disobedience of the triumvirate's instructions, gave the critics a point of attack. It also meant that the military crisis, which had made possible his brief term of almost dictatorial power, was over. A military uprising led by San Martín and Alvear, and possibly inspired by the Masonic lodge with which Rivadavia had refused to cooperate, brought a new triumvirate to power and Rivadavia's return to private life for two years.

In 1814 he was sent with Belgrano on a complicated diplomatic mission to England and Spain which kept him in Europe for six years. In cooperation with Sarratea, the Argentine representative in London, they were to attempt to reach an agreement with the newly restored Spanish monarch, Ferdinand, for a constitutional regime in Argentina. Failing this, they were to seek in other European courts for protection and for a prince to serve as constitutional monarch. Another envoy soon joined them with special instructions to seek the protection of the British government. Since Argentina was independent in fact but still legally loyal to King Ferdinand, and since England was an ally of Spain, these negotiations were extremely delicate and complicated. Rivadavia went directly to Spain but failed to secure any agreement. Belgrano and the others were no more successful in England. The search for a European prince proved just as futile. As a result of these years in Europe, Rivadavia was more than ever convinced that a constitutional monarchy for Argentina was impossible, and he returned to his country a confirmed republican. He had made the acquaintance of Jeremy Bentham, Baron von Humboldt, Madame de Staël, and many others who had helped to crystallize his political ideas, and came back to his native country with clear conceptions of the importance of strong, centralized, responsible, and representative government.

The government in Buenos Aires had gone through an especially critical period of anarchy and civil war in 1820 which had swept away the institutions of national government, leaving the provinces autonomous, bound together only by an agreement to establish a federal constitution. Martín Rodríguez was governor of the province of Buenos Aires, and early in 1821 Rivadavia returned to become one of the two ministers of state in his government.

It was in this post that Rivadavia achieved his greatest success. His influence was felt in legislative reforms which opened the meetings of the legislature to the public and provided for the opening of sessions with an annual message, for the participation of ministers in the debates, and for the presentation of a budget by the executive. Ecclesiastical reforms adopted at this time included abolition of the *fuero,* or benefit of clergy, and various measures regulating the religious orders. These measures brought strong protests and threats of revolt, which were suppressed. The properties of the Brotherhood of Holy Charity were brought under government control and a voluntary Society of Beneficence was organized, with his encouragement, by society women of Buenos Aires to perfect morality, cultivate the spirit of the fair sex, and dedicate women to social service. Yet Rivadavia was not in any sense antireligious. On the contrary, this interest in reform was animated by deep religious conviction. The University of Buenos Aires, which Pueyrredón had initiated, was established in 1821 as the center of a national system of education. University scholarships for children from the other provinces was one of the farsighted provisions of this plan, which also included the creation of chairs of law and political science and the establishment of a college of moral sciences and an academy of medicine. Primary schools, released from control by the *cabildo*, were brought under the direction of this University. New elementary schools were established, especially in rural areas, so that the total number in the province grew from sixteen in 1821 to one hundred in 1826.

Rivadavia's concept of the State may be described as one of a militant state of ideals, "a doctrine in action" [1] which sought to achieve the embodiment of its ideals in political action. Although he was still the dispassionate leader of a decade earlier, just as averse as ever to demagogic agitation and political partisanship, and especially to the personalism of the current political scene, still, his political philosophy drove him to an increasingly clearcut program of radical reform. Unfortunately, this program had the effect of driving deeper the rift between Buenos Aires and the other provinces which had become so evident in the civil disturbances of 1820.

One of Rivadavia's most controversial measures was the suppression of the *cabildo* of Buenos Aires. This city council was a heritage from the colonial government, as had been noted. It combined legislative, judicial, and executive functions in the Spanish manner. Although it had taken an active part in the May Revolution, it had been largely forced to these actions by popular pressure. In its own constitution it was scarcely a democratic institution, since its offices were largely in the hands of the local nobility. In 1811 Rivadavia had strengthened the *cabildo's* position by seeking its support in his struggle with the junta. The *cabildo* had become increasingly assertive of its right to be consulted on every important measure. Moreover, it was constantly suspected of being the center of conspiracies againt the government. Suppression of the *cabildo* was probably necessary as a measure to protect the government against reactionary uprisings, yet it was unfortunate insofar as it removed a powerful counterpoise to the growing centralist tendencies of the Buenos Aires government. The example of

[1] Dana Montaño, Salvador M. *Las ideas políticas de Bernardino Rivadavia.* Santa Fe, Argentina, Universidad Nacional del Litoral. 1945. p23.

Buenos Aires was followed by the other provinces. The *caudillo* [2] governors welcomed the chance to get rid of an institution representing chiefly the old families of wealth and position who frequently opposed their wishes. As a result, there was no municipal self-government in Argentina for thirty years after suppression of the *cabildo*.

Another of his political reforms, the adoption of universal suffrage, was later criticized by Juan B. Alberdi as bringing "the intervention of the mob (*chusma*) in the government." At first Rivadavia opposed plans for assembling a new constituent congress. But toward the end of his ministry he came to hope that a constitutional assembly would approve the reform program of Buenos Aires and adopt a strong central government capable of extending this program to the other provinces. He was, therefore, largely responsible for arranging the national congress which assembled in 1824.

The best known and most controversial of the Rivadavia reform measures is the Law of Emphyteusis, by which he tried at one stroke to strengthen the government's credit and develop a land system. Expansion of cattle raising was bringing a rapid advance of settlement into the Indian areas of the province. But the government was anxious to see this expansion accompanied by agricultural development to support a larger population and encourage immigration. The public lands of the province were still extensive, and they were encumbered to guarantee a loan of 3 million pesos (1822) in London to build a harbor in Buenos Aires, establish a municipal water supply, and found three harbors on the southern coast. The terms of the loan prohibited sale of the lands, but, by the Law of Emphyteusis, they were rented for terms of at least twenty years. Rents were to be fixed by juries of appraisal every ten years. To encourage the production of cereal crops, rents on lands used for this purpose were fixed at the rate of 4 per cent per year, while lands used for pastoral purposes paid 8 per cent. Ownership remained in the hands of the government which presumably was to receive a considerable part of the increase in land values through increased rents based on decennial appraisals.

Extensive grants of land were made under this system during the 1820's, ranging from small grants of less than a square league to grants exceeding twenty square leagues. It was severely criticized by the cattle raisers of the province who preferred a system of outright sale, and who also objected to grants made to foreigners under the law. It was also a source of apprehension in the other provinces who saw in this system of Buenos Aires the prototype of a land system to be applied on a national scale if a centralized government were established in the metropolis. Later, under the Rosas dictatorship, the system was greatly restricted and ultimately fell into disuse.

[2] This term, meaning chief or leader, refers here to the petty, local military bosses or strong men who assumed political power during the breakdown of political institutions following independence. Frequently they were mestizos.

After the expiration of the term of the Rodríguez government in 1824, Rivadavia refused the offer to continue as minister under the new governor, Juan Gregorio de las Heras, and departed for Europe before the meeting of the federal constituent congress in December. For a year this congress devoted its sessions to immediate problems without formulating a constitution. Outbreak of war with Brazil, however, in which Argentina supported the cause of the "33" patriots who undertook to liberate Uruguay from Brazilian control, made a unified government imperative. It was already the habit to look to the governor of the province of Buenos Aires for leadership, especially in international difficulties. The congress therefore placed the executive power provisionally in the hands of Governor Las Heras in January 1825, even before determining what kind of executive the new nation should have. He soon attempted to resign this provisional power on the grounds that the nation should have an independent executive. The congress refused to accept his resignation, but a few months later adopted a law providing for a president and elected Rivadavia to the office.

One of the first moves of his administration was to federalize the city of Buenos Aires. The relationship of the capital city to the rest of the nation had been a perplexing problem for fifteen years, and it was to be fifty-five years more until a final solution was found. The measure adopted by the congress, nationalizing the capital, remained in effect only as long as Rivadavia remained president. The law placed the national capital under the direct rule of the president and the congress. The remainder of the province of Buenos Aires was to be constituted a separate province, but meanwhile, it too was ruled by the national government. Opposition to the change appeared at once in the provincial legislature, but Rivadavia dissolved the legislature and removed Governor Las Heras from his office. The latter accepted the change without resistance and soon departed for Chile, where he remained until his death in 1866. This effort to nationalize the capital city may have been a grave political mistake at the time, since it alienated the support of influential leaders and groups in the province of Buenos Aires. Yet it was like Rivadavia not to temporize, but to seek a radical solution of any problem he faced. Moreover, the solution which he proposed in this case, and got the congress to adopt, was the same solution which was ultimately adopted later after half a century of dispute.

In spite of divided opinion in the congress and the well-known opposition of many of the provincial governors, a centralized constitution was drawn up and submitted to the provinces for approval. Six provinces declared they would not accept this centralized constitution, and only the war with Brazil prevented an immediate breakup of the union. Even the war could not prevent the open opposition of such chieftains as Bustos and Quiroga, and Rivadavia welcomed the British offer of mediation to end the war with Brazil, believing a successful settlement would strengthen his hand for dealing with the opposition. He was wrong. Manuel J. García, who was sent to Rio de Janeiro to negotiate the peace, went beyond his instructions and signed a treaty annexing Uruguay to Brazil. This action brought on a political crisis, and while both the president and congress disavowed the treaty, Rivadavia felt it necessary to resign in light of the whole political situation. His successor dissolved the constituent congress, whose work was now a failure, restored the autonomy of the province of Buenos Aires, and assembled representatives of that province to choose a new governor.

Thus the brief and ill-starred term of the first president of Argentina came to a premature end. His brilliant administration had given brief promise of the achievement of democratic, stable government in anarchic Argentina. But he was a man ahead of his times. His far-reaching plans for political reorganization and his measures of liberal social and economic reform drove deeper the already deep three-sided split between the metropolis, the rural areas of Buenos Aires, and the other provinces. His supporters at the best were never very numerous, and for the time being they were completely defeated by reaction in the provinces and by the hostility of the ranchers of Buenos Aires. Rivadavia departed to spend the rest of his life in Europe in exile. He died in Cadiz in 1845.

His downfall had been due to distrust of his far-reaching reforms, opposition to his centralist constitution, and miscarriage of the negotiations with Brazil. The war against Brazil had worked temporarily to unite the provinces, and its successful conclusion represented his best hope for success. García's "betrayal" may have been partly due to Rivadavia's seeking to end the war prematurely. If so, it was not the first time that Rivadavia had misjudged a military and diplomatic situation. A few years before he had given his approval to the Buenos Aires congress in its refusal to grant additional supplies to San Martín, believing that the war was over and should be ended by treaty. When Belgrano won his striking victory over the Spaniards at Tucumán it was in violation of Rivadavia's orders. It was, perhaps, a similar mistake in misjudging the situation in the war with Brazil which brought about Rivadavia's downfall.

He had become so embittered toward his country that in his will he forbade taking his body back to Argentina. But his remains today lie in a sumptuous mausoleum in the heart of Buenos Aires, and on September 2, 1945, Argentina celebrated the centennial of this great civilian leader, first president of the republic and one of its earliest liberal leaders. The ideals for which he stood were greater than the frustrations, mistakes, and disappointments of his career. Upon resigning the presidency he is reported to have said: "I am reason and I do not wish to be force." Thus, even in defeat he lived up to his ideal of democratic leadership. But Argentina had to endure two decades of reaction, frustration, and terror under the dictatorship of Juan Manuel Rosas before a new generation of political leaders appeared to resume Rivadavia's mantle. Bartolomé Mitre, Domingo

F. Sarmiento, Juan B. Alberdi, and Nicolás Avellaneda, youths just entering upon manhood at the time of his overthrow, profited from his experience. They, at last, were able to rise above the division between Unitarists and Federalists and to continue the lines of political, economic, and educational advance presaged by the first president.

Abud, Salomón. Rivadavia, el organizador de la república. Buenos Aires. Claridad. 1945. 508p.

Burgin, Miron. Economic aspects of Argentine federalism, 1820-1852. (Harvard economic studies, no. 78) Cambridge, Harvard University Press. 1946. 304p.

Capdevila, Arturo. Rivadavia y el españolismo liberal de la revolucíon argentina. Buenos Aires, Ateneo. 1931. 268p.

Cuadernos americanos. 4, no. 6:149-60. November-December 1945. Rivadavia. Angel Ossorio.

Dana Montaño, Salvador M. Las ideas políticas de Bernardino Rivadavia. Santa Fe, Argentina, Universidad Nacional del Litoral. 1945. 104p.

Galván Moreno, C. Rivadavia, el estadista genial; reseña documentada de su vida y su obra. Buenos Aires, Claridad. 1940. 582p.

Levene, Ricardo. A history of Argentina. (Tr. and ed. by William Spence Robertson) (Inter-American historical series, v 1) Chapel Hill, University of North Carolina Press. 1937. 565p. Especially ch. 30, 39-42.

Wilgus, A. Curtis, ed. South American dictators during the first century of independence. (Studies in Hispanic American affairs, v5) Washington, D.C., George Washington University Press. 1937. p78-91. Bernardino Rivadavia, Argentine dictator and institution builder. L. W. Bealer.

DIOGO ANTÔNIO FEIJÓ (1784-1843)

REGENT OF BRAZIL

The political career of Diogo Antônio Feijó shows in many ways the characteristics which have distinguished political life in Brazil from that of the Spanish American republics—characteristics such as the achievement of reforms within the structure of monarchy; the avoidance of a fatal rift between reforming leadership and the church; the tendency for moderate liberals committed to maintaining order to triumph over more radical liberal leadership. Only through great flexibility and accomodation on the part of Brazilian political leaders were the greatly disparate sections of Brazilian economy and politics held together during the trying days of Pedro I and the Regency. The greatness of the Brazilian leaders stands out in striking contrast against the background of the political fragmentation which was going on all around them in Spanish America.

Feijó was of a particularly intransigent character, and this quality sharply differentiates him from the other leaders of his day. Yet it would be difficult to find among the leaders produced by the operation of the strong and frequently contradictory forces of Brazilian national life a figure more characteristic in other aspects than this liberal São Paulo priest.

Union in Brazil was favored by strong economic forces. Brazil, in this respect, was like the early United States in being a union of seaboard colonies, united by interest in growing export trade. During the seventeenth century, on their own initiative, the Portuguese colonists had driven out the Dutch. Transfer of the seat of the Portuguese empire to Brazil during the Napoleonic wars had given Brazilians another experience in united action. British policy and early Portuguese recognition of Brazilian independence were additional favorable factors. Yet the rapidly changing character of Brazilian economy was reflected in changeable politics; and the generally unsettled character of the country's political life until the middle of the nineteenth century called for talents of political leadership of the highest order if the union was to be maintained.

The language of Brazilian partisan politics has usually been violent. In contemporary accounts, therefore, Feijó appears either as a monster or as a paragon of all the political virtues. His fundamental objectives and motives have been obscured by the heat of controversy. Even from the vantage point of history it is difficult to make them entirely intelligible. But the true Feijó, whether as deputy in the Cortes of Lisbon, as regent of the empire, or as leader of the São Paulo rebellion of 1842, was consistently incorruptible, courageous, unyielding. He was a defender of liberal monarchy, and a spokesman for those elements in Brazilian society which wanted to see the new broom sweep clean in a thoroughgoing reform of government, army, church, and education. But for him respect for law and order was a necessary concomitant to any reforms. There could be no trifling with libertarian disorder. He was loyal to the monarchy even as a popularly elected regent. Although an outstanding advocate of clerical reform, he remained loyal to the church, a pious priest with a strain of mysticism derived from his association with the community of Itú, the Port Royal of Brazil.

Feijó was born in São Paulo in August 1784, the natural son of Maria Joaquina de Camargo. The Camargo family was one of the rich and politically powerful landowning families of São Paulo. The identity of his father was a carefully guarded family secret. Probably it was Manoel de la Cruz Lima, who became a canon in the Council of the Diocese of São Paulo in 1788. But it may have been Manoel's brother, also a priest, João Gonçalves Lima, who was Diogo's godfather. His illegitimate birth later was to be an important motive for his vigorous and persistent campaign to abolish the rule of clerical celibacy in Brazil.

His early years were spent with his mother in the large Camargo household on the Rua da Freira in São Paulo, and in general he was brought up there. But much of his early education was received from his godfather, Padre João Gonçalves Lima, whom he accompanied to Guaratinguetá and later to Parnaíba. His godfather taught him Latin and in Guaratinguetá arranged for him to study with the distinguished teacher, Licenciado Manoel Gonçalves Franco. At the age of seventeen he was studying rhetoric with Estanislau José de Oliveira in São Paulo, but for the most part he seems to have continued his studies with his godfather in Parnaíba until 1803.

In 1804 he was admitted to minor religious orders as a subdeacon, and established himself as a teacher of Latin and Portuguese grammar in the village of São Carlos, north of São Paulo. Here he lived a life of solitude and poverty, supporting a household which consisted of the faithful family slave, Agostinho, and a young apprentice, Modesto. He had a small income from teaching, but seems to have depended in part on charity. At this time he was greatly tormented by thoughts of his illegitimate origin, which he knew had delayed his receiving regular orders, and which he was compelled to denounce for this purpose. Yet, as so often happens, the solitude and the moral crisis through which he was passing seemed to develop his self confidence and strength of character. That he was far from idle during these years is shown by the fact that he composed a Latin grammar while finishing his preparation for the priesthood. He was ordained in December 1808 at the age of twenty-four, and received a minor church appointment in São Paulo, but he preferred to return to the solitude of São Carlos.

There he spent the next ten years of his life, until 1818, as a teacher, priest, and planter. On the death of his grandfather, his mother's generosity enabled him to acquire a small sugar plantation. He became a prosperous farmer, building a sugar mill and producing sugar and rum. His household now consisted of thirteen slaves, including the faithful Agostinho and two apprentices. He continued his teaching, however, and composed a book of rhetoric during this period for his students. He also said mass regularly, preached, and heard confessions. It was during these years that the charge was made that he had seduced a young woman in the confessional to become the mistress of another priest. The charge was made, strangely enough, by a man who was later to become one of Feijó's enthusiastic supporters. The accusation was groundless and Feijó was absolved; but the story persisted, and was later revived against him when he became a prominent figure in national politics. That he had become a person of consequence in São Carlos appears from his selection to preach the funeral sermon on the occasion of the death of Queen Maria (1818) and also the sermon celebrating the coronation of King João VI.

In the year 1818 he made a decision which was to determine his whole subsequent career. He renounced the life of a prosperous *fazendeiro*, left his sugar plantation, and joined the mystic, ascetic community of The Fathers of Protection (*Patrocinio*) at Itú. He was attracted to Itú especially by Padre Jesuino do Monte Carmelo. This mulatto priest, who was the outstanding leader of the Itú community, was a man of versatile talents, great energy and force of character, and of decidedly liberal political views. He was an architect, a painter, and a musician who had taken holy orders after the death of his wife. Under his leadership Itú was rapidly becoming known as the "Port Royal of Brazil," a center of clerical liberalism. But the seeds of a strong reforming interest must already have been well planted in Feijó's character for him to be drawn to such a group, and to assume at once, as he did, a prominent place in the life of Itú. He began at once to preach and to teach ideas there which were previously unknown in Brazil —especially the philosophy of Immanuel Kant. A compendium of moral philosophy and one of logic, composed at this time, clearly reflect these new interests.

The liberal revolution of 1820 in Portugal brought a call for the election of deputies to a Cortes in Lisbon. Feijó was named one of seven electors from that place to participate in the selection of the São Paulo deputies. In the provincial electoral junta he met the Andrada brothers, José Bonifacio,[1] Martim Francisco, and Antônio Carlos, representatives of the conservative landowner class in São Paulo, under whose influence the new provincial government had been set up. From this initial encounter came a

---

[1] See Harold E. Davis, *Makers of Democracy in Latin America.* p39-41.

feeling of antagonism between Feijó and the Andradas which was later to develop into one of the most significant divisions in Paulista and Brazilian politics. Feijó was one of the six São Paulo deputies elected. Antônio Carlos de Andrada was also one of the six.

Like the other Brazilian deputies, Feijó took little active part in the meetings of the Cortes, because of the atmosphere of hostility in which the Brazilians found themselves. He quickly became disgusted with the narrowness and suspicion of the Portuguese, and adopted a policy of watching and listening. His only speech, on April 25, 1822, declared for complete autonomy of the states of Brazil. When a Brazilian commission proposed, as a basis of conciliation, that a separate parliament be set up for Brazil, with a delegation of royal authority, he refused to follow the leadership of Antônio Carlos Andrada in supporting the proposal. With Antônio Carlos he later refused to sign the constitution drawn up, and escaped with seven other Brazilian deputies on the English packet *Marlborough*. Back in Brazil he promptly made known his support of the independence and union of Brazil under a limited representative monarchy.

Feijó was elected a substitute member of the Brazilian constitutional assembly, but had no opportunity to serve before it was dissolved by the emperor in 1823. When Pedro proposed his own constitution in 1824, Feijó was the moving spirit in an Itú junta which formulated criticisms and suggested amendments. They advocated further limitations on the powers of the emperor, abolition of his power to dissolve the assembly, more autonomy for the provinces, and limitations on the freedom of the press. These views caused him and his friends, Paula Sousa and Vergueiro, to be considered leaders of a party of "pernicious ideas." Yet he was elected a member of a legislative assembly which opened in 1826. In the assembly he joined with Evaristo, editor of the influential liberal journal, *Aurora fluminense*, and Bernardo Pereira de Vasconcellos, in advocating religious, educational, and political reforms. He urged abolition of the rule of celibacy, exclusion of foreign religious orders from Brazil, the superiority of civil over ecclesiastical authority, municipal reforms, reform of the system of local justice (justices of the peace), and codification of criminal law. He also advocated confiscation of the wealth of the religious orders in place of a loan to the Bank of Brazil. He had given up wearing clerical garb, and for this, too, he was criticized by more conservative clergy. The Englishman John Armitage, who was in Brazil at this time, commented on Feijó's "firmness of character" and soul: "He was singular in his opinions, tenacious in his projects, of little erudition, except in ecclesiastical matters, enjoyed a reputation of probity, and was of an ultra-republican simplicity of customs.[2]

[2] Armitage, John. *History of Brazil*, 2d ed. São Paulo. 1914. p166.

The nine-year reign of Pedro I was a troubled one, in which the emperor had shown little ability as a constitutional ruler. The highly centralized constitution which he had imposed on the country after dissolving the constituent congress in 1823, although democratic in many respects, was the source of criticism in the provinces which were jealous of their rights, as well as in the General Assembly, which chafed at the lack of ministerial responsibility.

In the years which followed, Pedro seemed able to rule neither with nor without the assembly. He vacillated between cabinets which might gain the confidence of the legislature and those drawn from his friends among the Portuguese who would support him in opposition to his congress. Military defeat in the Uruguayan War, which brought about the independence of that country from Brazil in 1828, dealt a severe blow to his prestige. No less important in alienating the loyalty of his subjects was the emperor's scandalous attachment for the Marchioness of Santos, whom he installed in a house next to the royal palace. The Empress Leopoldina was very popular, on the other hand, and when she died after a violent argument with Pedro over the Marchioness, many Brazilians blamed him for her death. Pedro's inheritance of the Portuguese crown in 1826 also made his political position more difficult. Even though he renounced the throne in favor of his daughter, Maria Gloriosa, it was clear that he could not avoid being drawn into Portuguese politics in the civil strife which broke out in that country. The Portuguese question also had the effect of identifying the emperor more closely than ever with the unpopular Portuguese element in Brazil. Yet while these circumstances undoubtedly made his position more and more difficult, the fundamental fault probably lay in his failure to play successfully the difficult role of a constitutional ruler.

On April 7, 1831 a revolution forced the abdication of Pedro I. A group of radicals, or *exaltados*, of republican tendencies began the movement, but they were soon joined by a group of moderates, including Feijó, Vasconcellos, and Evaristo. These moderates captured political control of the new government in the selection of the three-man regency. Neither the *exaltados* nor the friends of Pedro were well satisfied with this outcome, and uprisings and disorders throughout the country quickly threatened to dissolve the new regime in chaos. Pedro had not succeeded in stabilizing the political life of the nation, and his overthrow was the signal for a new outbreak of the forces of factionalism and particularism. The army officers were predominantly loyal to Pedro, while the rank and file were greatly stirred by republican agitation. There was widespread nativist dissatisfaction with trade policies which tied Brazil closely to Britain and Portugal, while the efforts of the government to carry out the provisions of the Treaty of 1826 for the suppression of the slave trade brought rebellion, especially in the northern provinces.

Feijó was named Minister of Justice under the Regency because of his reputation for courage and probity, and because of the strong position he had taken in congress in favor of maintaining order. During the next two years his vigorous measures, supported by the Sociedade Defensora da Liberdade e Independencia, the organization of the moderates, did much to bring the conditions of near anarchy under control. Volunteers were organized and a national guard established. He moved quickly to check a revolt of the 26th Infantry Battalion and the military police guard. An uprising of *exaltados* was likewise suppressed, and shortly afterward a revolt in which *exaltados* joined with conservatives. He was equally successful in dealing with a conservative (*Caramurú*) revolt in 1832 which aimed at restoration of Pedro I.

His firmness and courage in dealing with civil disorders clearly revealed him as a vigorous leader suited to the needs of a nation in time of crisis or revolution. But he was less successful in securing from a faction-ridden congress the constructive measures of reform he deemed necessary. The standing army was reduced, but the congress refused to enact the measures Feijó demanded for reform of the army, the criminal code, and the magistracy, or to provide adequately for organization of the national guard. His demand for adequate measures to suppress the slave trade split the moderate party, tending to drive some of the moderates into cooperation with the disgruntled *exaltados*, and, sometimes, with the conservative (*Caramurú*) followers of José Bonifacio.[3] The failure of the congress to pass the necessary measures was not due to Feijó alone, of course. It stemmed in part from the political weakness of the three-man regency. Convinced that the measures to achieve the stabilization of the nation's political life could be achieved only through constitutional reform, he tried to have the chamber of deputies declare itself a national assembly to reform the constitution. When this move was blocked by some of the moderates led by Honorio Hermeto, he resigned. Interestingly enough, his resignation had the effect of forcing the enactment of the law authorizing the next legislative assembly to amend the constitution.

Leaving Rio, he returned to São Paulo, making no effort to defend himself from the bitter attacks launched against his ministry in the chamber of deputies. But his retirement was brief. The moderates of Rio de Janeiro elected him to the senate, where he launched at once into a vigorous campaign for the reform measures he had urged as minister. He proposed reform of the provincial governments and reform of the magistracy (justices

---

[3] This conservative party derived its unusual name from the picturesque sixteenth-century Diogo Alvares, who had taken the Indian name of Caramarú after being shipwrecked on the coast of Bahia in 1510. The natives made him a "king," and he married several Indian women. In 1549 he welcomed and assisted the colonizing expedition of Tomé de Souza, and he and his descendants took a prominent part in the development of the colony. To trace one's ancestry back to Caramarú in Brazil is like being a descendant of Pocahontas in the United States.

of the peace). He discussed the proposed new criminal code, insisting on a liberal definition of habeas corpus.

Meanwhile, in November 1834, he began the publication of a journal, *O justiçeiro*. *O justiçeiro* was not a financial success and soon died. But from its pages emerges a clear picture of the program of reform which made Feijó the center of so much of the political controversy of these years. He urged the abolition of the life term in the senate, abolition of the nobility, reform of justice, elimination of nepotism, clerical reform, and reform of the army. He foresaw for Brazil a monarchy without a nobility, in which the regent (under the reform of the constitution which had been adopted in 1834) would be "somewhat less than the president of the United States." "Eight or nine years are given us for experience," he wrote, referring to the period which would elapse until the young monarch, Pedro II, reached his majority. Only two parties remained in Brazil, he argued, the moderates and the conservative *restauradores* (Caramurú), and he called for support of the moderates.

Feijó was elected regent in 1835 under the constitutional reform of the preceding year which provided a single regent. He was elected by the votes of the moderates. But the extent to which the party of the moderates had split appeared in the fact that he secured only a plurality of the votes of the electoral juntas. Vasconcellos, his firm collaborator in the moderate ministry in 1832, was one of his principal opponents in the contest for the regency. That this was more than an intra-party dispute quickly appeared as Vasconcellos and other moderates began consistent opposition to Feijó in cooperation with the conservative *Caramurús*, especially after the death of Pedro I in 1834 removed the supposed threat of his restoration.

The single regency, under Feijó, from 1835 to 1837, and under his successor, Pedro de Araujo Lima, from 1837 to 1840, was in many respects an experiment in republican government under the guise of a regency. Feijó, as we have seen, realized that this was so, and that only a limited time was given to Brazil to establish the basic lines of its constitutional government. Yet, while his regency redounded to his personal credit as a political leader of firmness, foresight, and probity, it was far from successful in the fundamental task of welding the disparate and dissenting elements of the Brazilian political scene into an instrument for effective, progressive action such as he desired. His unyielding demands for essential reforms alarmed the increasingly conservative political majority in congress who represented the interests of slave-owning *fazendeiros*, and who were convinced that change had already gone too far. His refusal to organize a government on the principle of ministerial responsibility to that majority produced a political stalemate which proved fatal to his other efforts, while giving his conservative opponents the opportunity to attack him as an opponent of liberal government.

The problems of his regency were many and serious. The Negro slave trade in Brazil continued apace, and Feijó's efforts to secure measures to enforce suppression of the trade and his move to renew the trade treaty of 1827 with Britain, which was about to expire, raised a political storm which prevented any constructive action on other matters. A dispute with the Papacy over the establishment of two new bishoprics and over the appointment of the Bishop of Rio de Janeiro was further complicated by proposals which were being urged in Brazil for the establishment of civil marriage, and by Feijó's advocacy of the abolition of the rule of celibacy. His administration faced rebellions in Rio Grande do Sul and in the province of Pará. Congress refused to approve the measures necessary to deal effectively with these civil disturbances. Like the refusal to enact his other reform measures, this refusal was due in considerable degree to his stubborn opposition to the appointment of a conservative ministry. He believed that the constitution of Brazil required that the regent rule as well as reign. On this he refused to compromise. He was equally adamant against resorting to unconstitutional measures to meet the increasing difficulties of his administration. The congressional election of 1836 was a clear victory for the coalition of conservative leaders in congress, and the intensified opposition of this group brought Feijó's resignation in September, 1837.

After a period of retirement he returned to the senate, of which he was elected president in 1839. From this position he continued vigorous advocacy of judicial, educational, and clerical reforms. He was an active participant in the move, which had its origin in liberal sources, to declare the majority of the young emperor. The liberal domination of the new government was short-lived, however, and after the new triumph of the conservatives, Feijó returned to his retirement in São Carlos.

The last chapter of his life was an anticlimax. Sick and half paralyzed, disillusioned and pessimistic, he nevertheless joined an uprising of São Paulo liberals in 1842. The revolution was a protest against the conservative (regresso) ministry, then in power, which had dissolved, even before it had met, the liberal congress elected in 1842. There were undoubtedly some grounds for the conservatives' claim that the preceding liberal ministry had controlled the elections in its own interest, but Feijó and his liberal friends were convinced that the conservatives intended to maintain themselves in power indefinitely by unconstitutional means. The rebellion developed in the provinces of São Paulo and Minas Gerais. It was quickly suppressed in both provinces, its leaders deserting the cause after an initial military reverse. Feijó, almost alone, held out to the end in São Paulo. Captured by the same General Luis Alves de Lima who had supported him loyally as Minister of Justice in 1832, he was imprisoned and exiled in Vitoria, the capital of Espirito Santo, from July to December 1842. He was returned to Rio early in 1843, and immediately resumed his place in the senate. Almost completely paralyzed as he was, and while the discussion over his punishment was still going on, he presented his own defense to the senate, and led a parliamentary attack on the ministry. The discussion of his case dragged on while he lay sick and dying. Even in this condition, he was a force to be reckoned with, and Honorio Hermeto and Bernardo Pereira de Vasconcellos, powerful directors of the conservatives in the senate, did not wish (or did not dare) to force a senate decision against the former regent.

At length he secured permission to return to São Paulo to await the senate's decision. Always a devout Christian, notwithstanding his ardent advocacy of church reform, he devoted his last days, in notable calm of spirit, to religious meditation and prayer. His death on November 10, 1843, removed one of the most vigorous and forthright leaders in the history of his nation. The circumstances of his death, with the decision of the senate still pending, had the effect of making him appear a martyr to the cause of Brazilian liberalism.

Although in his political career he experienced many notable defeats—on the whole more defeats than victories—he emerges from the history of the times as a strong, forceful character of great probity, who set a striking example of political action based upon principles. More than any other Brazilian leader of his day, he gave practical political expresssion to the insistent liberal demands for social and political reform. His attempt, as elected regent, to play a role comparable to that of the president of the United States was a failure in many respects. Yet the example of a regent attempting to give expression to what he conceived to be a national need for a constructive progressive program, even in opposition to a hostile majority of the congress, did much to prepare the way for the liberal monarchy of Pedro II.

Calogeras, João Pandiá. A history of Brazil. (Tr. and ed. by Percy A. Martin) (Inter-American historical series, v3) Chapel Hill, University of North Carolina Press. 1939. p 120-30 and *passim*.

Manchester, Alan K. British preëminence in Brazil. Chapel Hill, University of North Carolina Press. 1933. 371p.

Oliveira Lima, Manoel de. O imperio brasileiro, 1822-1889. São Paulo, Comp. Melhoramentos de São Paulo. 1927. 250p.

Sousa, Octavio Tarquinio de. Diogo Antônio Feijó (1784-1843) (Coleção documentos brasileiros, 35) Rio de Janeiro, J. Olympio. 1942. 332p.

FRANCISCO DE PAULA SANTANDER (1792-1840)

THE MAN OF LAW

The bitterness of political struggles in Latin America, and the consequent vilification of its political leaders has darkened the name of many men of outstanding merit who deserve better historical reputations. Because of his differences with Simón Bolívar, Santander almost suffered this fate. Some historians have unjustly made him the scapegoat for the failure of the Bolivarian plan for a Greater Colombia. On the other hand, members of the Centro de Historia de Santander, in recent years, have frequently gone too far in the opposite direction. Not only have they appropriately eulogized him as the great founding father of their nation, but they have tended to present him as a statesman without blemish, which he was not, and as the founder of Colombian liberalism, a distinction to which his claim is somewhat controversial. José M. Forero, a recent biographer, while still partial to Santander, represents a more balanced view in his recent remark that Colombia "received from Bolívar its existence and liberty, but to Santander it owes the first precepts and highest postulates of democracy."

Like so many others of his generation, his entire mature life, until his early death at forty-eight, was filled with the wars of independence and the founding of his native state. He outlived the revolutionary period only long enough to serve a term as president of New Granada and then, for a brief period following, a term in its house of representatives. During his early years he supported the ecclesiastical, social, and educational reforms of Bolívar. His break with the Liberator was due to a number of causes, but among them may be noted his opposition to the "monarchical" tendencies of the constitutional reforms the latter was trying to secure from the Convention of Ocaña in 1828 and his open criticism of the Bolivarian dictatorship of that year. In opposition to Bolívar's plan for a centralized state with a powerful executive, Santander urged the federal principle of organization which would have left Venezuela, New Granada,[1] and Ecuador considerable autonomy. He also favored a weaker executive, with more power left in the hands of congress.

His conflict with Bolívar was not part of a quarrel between reform and conservatism. Both men were reformers. Perhaps, though, Santander's ad-

[1] New Granada was the name given to the area of the present-day republic of Colombia by its conqueror, Quesada, in the sixteenth century. In the eighteenth century it was part of the viceroyalty which included the present-day republics of Ecuador and Venezuela as well. The first independent government organized in what is now Colombia, in 1810, bore the name of New Granada. With the breakup of Bolívar's Gran Colombia, as will be noted, New Granada reasserted its independence in 1831, retaining its original name. In 1858 it became the Granadine Confederation, and in 1861 Colombia.

vocacy of the federal principle gave some of the forces of social conservatism an opportunity to defeat the Liberator's plans. The year 1828 was a crucial year in the relations of Santander and Bolívar, as well as in the history of Greater Colombia. Throughout Latin America a reaction against the initial liberal enthusiasm of the revolution was gaining force. Although leader of a group advocating "liberal" principles during the succeeding twelve years, Santander represented this change in New Granada. It is significant, too, that many of his followers were later to be found in the grouping of conservative party forces through which Colombia's political life was stabilized in the mid-nineteenth century, although Santander was not the founder of the party.

Marshal Sucre accused both him and Bolívar of "localism," that is, favoring the local interests of New Granada and Venezuela, respectively. The unfortunate rift between the two was a split between two groups of Colombian revolutionary leaders, a split caused by personalities, regional jealousies, and differences over measures more than principles. The two men were as different as could be. Santander, in Bolívar's own words was the "man of laws," the ablest political administrator of the Bolivarian movement, the man who saw how to translate into laws and institutions the reforms of the revolutionary era. Bolívar was the revolutionary leader *par excellence,* a rare combination of military and political genius. Yet, for all his realistic understanding of the basis of Latin American political life, Bolívar was inept as an administrator. The tragedy of the meteoric Bolivarian Greater Colombia, which shone with a transient brilliance on the Latin American horizon until Bolívar's disappearance from the political scene, centers around the failure of these two leaders to agree after Bolívar's return from Peru in 1827.

Santander's family was typical of that of many prosperous creole leaders of the independence movements. Through his father he was descended from Don Francisco Martínez de Rivamontán y Santander, Knight of Santiago, who came to New Granada in 1612 as governor. His mother was the "illustrious" Doña Manuela de Omaña y Rodríguez, an Indian princess. His father had been governor of the Province of San Faustino de los Rios. A rich landowner, and the owner of many slaves, he had shown his sympathy with the cause of independence by supporting the revolt of the *comuneros* of Socorro, which occurred during the days of the war of the North American Revolution.

Francisco was born April 2, 1792, and spent his early years in the beautiful family villa in Rosario de Cúcuta. There, in a subtropical climate, under the shade of cacao and coconut trees, he grew up, his days given to games, horseback riding, and other pursuits of rural life, and to scholarly exercises under the direction of a tutor—the life typical of the son of a prosperous and aristocratic creole family. At the age of thirteen he was sent to Bogotá to the Colegio de San Bartolomé, where he studied under his uncle, Nicolás Omaña. From him, Santander later declared, he learned "the justice, convenience, and necessity of his country escaping from Spanish domination."

He was just completing the study of law in 1810. This was the year in which revolutionary juntas throughout Spanish America assumed direction of their own affairs in the name of the deposed King Ferdinand VII, giving great impetus to the revolutionary movement. Santander, who was then eighteen, immediately enlisted in the revolutionary forces, in a regiment made up of the youth of many of the leading families of Bogotá. Soon he became secretary of the junta of Marquita and quickly rose to the military rank of captain.

Although only a junior officer, he inevitably became involved in the civil strife which now split the patriot forces of New Granada, dividing and nullifying their efforts during the early years of the independence movement. The first constitution of New Granada provided for a union of all the provinces on federal principles. But this was shortly replaced by the more centralist constitution of 1813 under President Antonio Nariño. The other provinces, jealous of the dominant role of Bogotá and its province of Cundinamarca under this second constitution, formed the United Provinces of New Granada, a government in which Camilo Torres soon became an outstanding figure. New Granada was thus divided by civil strife and war just at the time when every effort should have been directed toward preparation for resisting the army coming from Spain under General Pablo Morillo to restore royal authority. Santander joined with the federalists under Antonio Baraya in 1812, and took part under Baraya's leadership in the latter's defeat of the forces of Nariño at Ventaquemada, and in the later unsuccessful siege of Bogotá.

Meanwhile, Bolívar appearing in New Granada after the overthrow of Miranda's short-lived Venezuelan republic, enlisted the support of New Granada in reconquering Venezuela from the Spaniards. One of the first meetings of Santander and Bolívar resulted in a clash of their two strong wills. The incident occurred at Angostura de la Grita. Santander, and his commander, Colonel Castillo, had been placed under Bolívar's orders, but opposed his plans for a Venezuelan campaign. When Castillo refused to carry out the marching orders of the Liberator, he was removed, leaving Santander in command. Santander, loyal to his commanding officer, likewise refused to obey. Infuriated, Bolívar faced the young captain: "March immediately," he ordered. "There is no alternative. You march or shoot me, or positively, I will shoot you." Santander complied, and from that day until the fatal political rift in 1828, remained a faithful follower and colleague of the Liberator.

Bolívar was defeated in this Venezuelan campaign, and soon retired to the island of Jamaica to await a better opportunity. His defeat at this time, together with the internecine strife among the New Granadinians, opened the way for Morillo's reconquest of the country in the battle of Cachirí in 1816. Meanwhile Santander had become second in command of the forces of New Granada. After the royalist occupation of Bogotá he retired, with a small force of guerrillas, to the plains in the valley of Apure (present-day Venezuela). Shortly after his arrival there he was forced to give up his command to the eccentric Venezuelan, José Antonio Páez, idol of the Venezuelan llaneros, or cowboys. But he cooperated loyally with Páez, and, together, they laid the basis of the army which was soon to liberate New Granada once more from Spanish rule.

Santander was not, by temperament, a natural leader for these rough, hard-riding llaneros. To them he was a "general of the pen." His corpulence also deprived him of grace and dignity in movement, especially in comparison with the dashing Páez. Average in stature, he was light in complexion, with a small forehead, which sloped backwards and was surmounted by a mass of straight chestnut-colored hair. A straight nose, narrow lips, deep-set and penetrating grey eyes, a short beard, and a generally grave expression combined, however, to give him an air of energy and resolution.

This was the young man of twenty-five who in 1817 became one of Bolívar's principal lieutenants in the campaign to liberate New Granada. During 1816 and 1817 the little band of seven hundred ill-equipped patriots in the Apure Valley had gained many successes against the much larger and better equipped royalist forces. The campaign of Apure is one of which Colombians and Venezuelans still write and speak with great patriotic pride. Their successes might have been greater had not disorders among the patriots, resulting in the assassination of several of their leaders, been poorly held in check by General Páez. However, Bolívar's return to Venezuela in 1817 with a new expedition galvanized their forces into really effective action. Páez remained the chief leader in Venezuela, while Santander, as leader of the forces of New Granada, quickly assumed a prominent position in the campaign launched against New Granada from Venezuelan soil. With General Carlos Soublette he shared the direction of Bolívar's general staff. He took part in the initial campaign against San Fernando, and in the patriot victory at Calabozo in March 1818. The following month, when Bolívar's forces were surprised by a detachment of royalist troops, it was Santander's timely warning which probably saved the Liberator's life. He rapidly won Bolívar's confidence as an administrator and became the latter's chief lieutenant in the affairs of New Granada. Since he was not the most distinguished leader among the New Granadinians, at this time, his selection by Bolívar, an unusually good judge of men, was all the more significant.

In June 1819 Bolívar began the arduous invasion of New Granada, across the Andes, by way of Chita. The difficulties of the half-naked Venezuelan plainsmen in this grueling passage across the freezing mountain heights almost beggar description. One of the greatest difficulties for the *llaneros* was that their horses could not be used on the mountain passes, and a *llanero* afoot felt himself only half a man. Only the indomitable will and courage of their leaders kept them going. Santander showed himself a great leader in this campaign. It was he who led the attack which opened the pass at Paya on June 27 and made possible the decisive patriot victory at Boyacá in August.

In 1819 Bolívar hastily assembled a congress at Angostura which ratified his plan for the union of Venezuela, Colombia, and Ecuador into Greater Colombia. Bolívar was made president, while Páez was named vice president in charge of Venezuela and Santander in Cundinamarca (present-day Colombia). Bolívar stopped in Bogotá only a few days to establish the new government and then continued his military campaign. Leaving the administration in the hands of Santander, he said: "I leave you in Santander another Bolívar."

Santander faced a tremendous task. Legislative and executive organization was completely lacking. The governments of 1810 and following years had been dictatorial even though libertarian. The heritage of civil strife made many of the people of New Granada apprehensive that reestablishment of the republic would bring a return to the disorders of the previous years. Although Boyacá was felt to have been a decisive victory, royalist armies were still occupying much of the country and royalist sentiment was still strong. The only congress in the republic until the congress of Cúcuta was assembled two years later was that of Venezuela. Amidst all these difficulties Santander had to establish a government which would accept the Bolivarian proposal of a Greater Colombia and meet the constantly growing demands of the Liberator for slaves who could earn their freedom by serving in the armies and for money to support these armies.

Santander has been greatly criticized for authorizing the execution of General Barreiro, commander of the Spanish forces at Boyacá, while negotiations were going on for the exchange of prisoners. The Spanish general, a professional soldier, had offered to serve in the forces of the republic, but was executed, presumably because he was plotting against the government. The execution of Barreiro was one of the mistakes of Santander's career, and while Bolívar supported him publicly, he is said to have censured him privately for this action.

In Santander's defense it is well to remember the precarious situation in which he found himself and the government of New Granada at this time. Since 1816 the viceroy had followed a policy of deliberate elimination of the leaders of Bogotá, such as Camilo Torres, who had supported the previous republic. Lack of this leadership and the deep-seated royalist sympathies of the city made its effective occupation by the republicans exceedingly difficult. Republican troops to enforce the occupation were few, since all were needed by Bolívar in his campaigns. Moreover, the royalists were still in force in many provinces. The provinces of the south were royalist in sympathy. The royalist leader in Popayán was in touch with the Captain General of Quito, Melchor Aymerich. A royalist army was in Rosario de Cúcuta, General Morillo was still operating, and the viceroy was in Cartagena with over two thousand troops. Under these circumstances it is not hard to see how Santander could have considered the execution of the royalist general an act necessary to consolidate the republicans' position, particularly if he was convinced that Barreiro was actually plotting a royalist uprising.

He sensed immediately that the success or failure of the union of Great Colombia was bound up with the career of the Liberator. The Republic of Colombia, he wrote, was "the only daughter (*hija única*) of the immortal Bolívar" and would succeed or fail with him. He knew moreover, that there was great opposition to the union in New Granada; and when Bolívar, in 1819, proposed a meeting of heads of families to ratify the union, Santander urged postponement. Yet two years later he held such an assembly and secured ratification of the union. In this assembly he made a special and successful plea for the cooperation of the clergy.

In the same year (1821) the congress of Cúcuta organized the republic and adopted a constitution for Great Colombia. Bolívar was elected president and Santander, vice president. The congress chose him in preference to Nariño, who had returned from exile to preside over the meetings of the congress, because the latter was considered too ambitious and too petulant. Santander's election was a recognition of two years of effective administration of the affairs of New Granada, and Bolívar in accepting the presidency made it clear that he intended to leave the administration in the hands of the vice president while he continued to wage war. The congress approved this arrangement. It also enacted a number of significant reforms. The slave trade was abolished, children of slave parents were granted freedom, and provision was made for the gradual liberation of the rest of the slave population, many of them half-caste. Freedom of press was established, and periodicals were exempted from postal dues. Generous provisions were made for establishing schools.

It was in carrying out these latter provisions that Santander made one of his most substantial contributions to his country's welfare. Indeed the history of public instruction in Colombia may almost be said to have commenced with him. As early as 1820 he had issued a decree which called for the establishment of a locally supported school in every town or village. These schools were to teach reading, writing, arithmetic, religious dogma,

Christian morality, and the rights and duties of man in society. Carrying out the provisions of the Congress of Cúcuta, he provided for continuation of the higher institutions already established in Bogotá, Caracas, Quito, Popayán and Mérida, and established new ones in Ibagué, Tunja, Medellín, Neiva, and elsewhere. He was criticized for introducing the study of Bentham's teachings on morals and legislation, even though they were carefully expurgated. On the other hand, he distributed 160,000 copies of a book on Catholic dogma, including the Decalog.

Although Bolívar, on occasion, accused him of "indifference" to demands for troops and funds to continue the war in Peru, Santander seems to have worked faithfully to meet these demands, which became increasingly great as the war moved on to its climax. Santander insisted upon working within the constitution and laws, and delays in meeting the Liberator's requests were usually the result of waiting for the congress to act. Bolívar, in fact, though irritated by the delays, later recognized the justice and statesmanship of Santander's course of action. After the victory at Ayacucho, which brought the long War of Independence to a close, Bolívar wrote to Santander in the most laudatory terms concerning the latter's whole course of action. It was in this letter that Bolívar appropriately referred to him as the "Man of Laws."

He was reelected for a second term as vice president in 1825. But the problems of this period were of a character quite different from those of the preceding years, and events took a different turn. The major problems were no longer those of waging a war for independence, but of consolidating a government on the basis of the wartime union established by Bolívar. Now that the war was over, the evils of personalism, localism, and militarism began to appear. In 1826 the Colombian senate removed General Páez from his position as head of the Department of Venezuela, and the Venezuelan revolt which followed was settled only by the personal intervention of Bolívar. Unfortunately, the settlement was one which seemed to many New Granadinians to place the Liberator on the side of the Venezuelans in opposition to Santander and the government of the united republic. Personal relations between the president and vice president were embittered from this time on, to the point where Bolívar wrote Santander "to save him the trouble of receiving his letters." Personal relations of the two men were further complicated by the fact that Bolívar was convinced that Santander had given support to revolution in Peru in January 1827.

Bolívar, now returned from Peru, resumed the presidency in September 1827, and events moved rapidly toward the short-lived Bolivarian dictatorship. Santander and his many followers were convinced that the only solution of the constitutional problem of the union lay in more federalism, while Bolívar was determined to secure a stronger, more centralized government.

Most historians agree that the failure of these two powerful leaders to reach an understanding at this time was a principal cause of the unfortunate Bolivarian dictatorship and its collapse. Bolívar himself admitted as much in a letter to General Rafael Urdaneta in 1830. The clash appeared openly in the congress of Ocaña (1828), where the federalist followers of Santander were in a majority and opposed the Liberator's constitutional plans. The congress finally agreed on a government with autonomous assemblies in each of the three major departments of the union, an unworkable arrangement which really satisfied no one. Bolívar soon felt impelled to assume dictatorial powers to deal with the growing disorders and suppressed by decree the powers of the vice president, making the break with Santander complete. The latter, on his part, made no secret of his opposition to the dictatorship, and continued to oppose Bolívar's plan.

To get him out of the country, Santander was appointed minister to the United States. But before his departure he became implicated in the September Conspiracy (1828), involving an attempted assassination of the dictator. He was arrested and tried with the other conspirators. How far he was actually involved in these acts of his friends is not entirely clear, but only the intervention of Bolívar saved him from execution. Bolívar's clemency may have been dictated in part by policy, but it also shows the great respect he continued to have for his former colleague. Santander reciprocated this respect. Two years later, from his exile in Paris, on learning of the Liberator's death, he wrote: "In America only the mean of spirit (*los miserables*) can rejoice at the death of Bolívar."

Near the end of 1831 a New Granada convention elected Santander President, inviting him to return from exile. He was president of the Republic from 1832 to 1836, years in which the difficult problems of adjusting relations with the two departing sister states of the union, Venezuela and Ecuador, were settled. With firmness, and at times with severity, he headed off separatist tendencies in Cauca, Antioquia, and the Magdalena Valley, and suppressed the conspiracy of July 1833 in which certain "Bolivarians" had joined with a group of reactionaries to oppose the liberal ideas and reforms of the government. One of the greatest problems of his administration was that of securing division of the debt of Greater Colombia between Venezuela, New Granada, and Ecuador. An equitable settlement was arranged, though not without giving rise to violent criticisms that the president had yielded too much to Venezuelan demands. The greatest achievements of his administration, however, were the preservation of order and the extension of the educational system of the country. To the latter, especially, he gave great attention.

His effort in 1836 to secure the election of General José María Obando as his successor failed. Since neither of the three presidential candidates won a majority in the election, congress chose Dr. José Ignacio Márquez, whom Santander considered an enemy although they were both of the liberal party which had overthrown the Bolivarian dictatorship. During his last years, until his death in 1840, he served as a deputy in the congress, participating in numerous bitter debates connected with the disorders of the Márquez administration, debates in which he was frequently the object of acrimonious charges against his conduct as president of the Republic.

Francisco de Paula Santander was the real founder of Colombia. For nearly twelve years of its crucial formative period he was in fact, if not all the time in title, its chief executive. "Man of Laws" and "Organizer of Victory," he laid the constitutional basis of the nation, organized its resources to make possible the continuation of the War of Independence, and carried out the liberal, democratic ideas of the Constitutions of 1821 and 1832. He was the founder of the system of public education in Colombia. He opposed the dictatorship of Bolívar in 1828 as unnecessary and undemocratic, while in his own conduct of national affairs he set a memorable example of a strong able administrator maintaining order against all threats, but acting within the laws of the country. The "liberal" reforms which he urged were moderate, indeed, in comparison with those of subsequent periods, or those then being advocated in other countries. It is particularly significant that Santander enjoyed the support of a large part of the clergy, in spite of measures which required the church to establish schools, or which expropriated church property for educational purposes.

Far from being a radical and visionary reformer, he was first and foremost a man of practical views, an administrator and organizer. It is somewhat pointless, therefore, to argue whether or not he was indeed a "Liberal." He was a revolutionist and subsequently a leader of the liberal party. But practical, workable measures always seemed to him more important than radical and visionary schemes. It is not surprising, therefore, to find some of his followers, in later years, among the conservative opponents of more radical programs of change.

Camacho Montoya, Guillermo. Santander, el hombre y el mito. Caracas, Cecilio Acosta. 1943. 238p.

Forero, José María. Santander. 3d. ed. Bogotá, Aguila. 1937. 248p.

Gómez Parra, Pedro. Santander, ensayo biográfico. (Biblioteca Santander, v 12) Bucaramanga, Colombia, Imp. del Departamento. 1940. 310p.

Henao, Jesús María, and Arrubla, Gerardo. History of Colombia. (Ed. and tr. by J. Fred Rippy) (Inter-American historical series, v2) Chapel Hill, University of North Carolina Press. 1938. 578p.

JOSÉ MANUEL BALMACEDA (1840-1891)

MILITANT REFORMER

The tragic career of the reformer president of Chile, Balmaceda, is still a subject of keen controversy among historians, as is the revolution which brought in its fatal denouement the political suicide of the defeated president. Joaquim Nabuco, the Brazilian statesman, while sympathetic with many of the reforms for which Balmaceda fought, inevitably interpreted his career in the light of the political crisis and dictatorship in Brazil during the first years of the Republic. He saw Balmaceda, therefore, as a demagogic dictator who betrayed the forces of progress and order in opposing the system of parliamentary government. Against his own class, the ruling class which, by 1890, had made Chile the most thriving and stable constitutional government in Spanish America, said Nabuco, Balmaceda seemed to raise all the destructive forces of chaos and disorder which had been the too-frequent curse of Latin American national life. For the first time, he says, a president of Chile led a revolution. He was "an evocation . . . in the presidency of Chile, of the South American genius for dictatorship which had never penetrated into that [country]." [1]

Yet to his followers, at the time, and since, Balmaceda has represented the climax of the rising tide of liberal reform in late nineteenth century Chile. The revolution of 1891, on the surface, was a conflict between the president and the congress over their respective constitutional powers. But behind this conflict, say the *Balmacedistas*, lay the fact that the president, making himself the champion of the masses of Chile, had embarked upon a program of liberal reforms which threatened the political and social position of the landowning oligarchy which had dominated Chilean life since the adoption of the conservative constitution of 1833. Balmaceda himself was a member of this class, and his political career as a reformer is therefore considered, according to the two opposing Chilean points of view, either a betrayal of his class and what it stood for (most of the substantial progress of Chile up to this time) or a striking example of the principle of *noblesse oblige.* The imputation of motives is always dangerous, but what we know of his personality seems to suggest the first of these two views. At least one of his biographers has presented him in that light—as a romantic reformer,

[1] Nabuco, Joaquim. *Balmaceda.* São Paulo, Companhia Editora Nacional and Rio de Janeiro, Civilizacão Brasileira S. A. 1937. 200p. See especially p13. The work appeared originally as a series of articles in the *Jornal de Comercio* in 1895, and was published as a book in same year in Rio de Janeiro and Valparaiso (Spanish translation). These articles were a commentary on, and an answer to, the two-volume book of Julio Bañados Espinosa, the colleague and literary legatee of Balmaceda, published in Paris in 1894, under the title *Balmaceda.* The two works should be read in conjunction.

who identified himself with the social interests of the underprivileged masses out of zealous devotion to certain causes and social ideas.[2]

José Manuel Balmaceda was born July 19, 1840 on the family hacienda, Bucalemu, in the extreme south of the Department of Melipilla, an hacienda whose shores were bathed by the rolling waves of the Pacific. He was the son of José Fernández de Balmaceda and María Encarnación Fernández. He was a scion of one of the old prominent families of the country. On his father's side, his grandfather had been a Spanish immigrant who took an active part, on the Chilean side, in the movement for independence. His father was a personal and political friend of the great Manuel Montt, Minister of Education, and soon to be president of the country. His mother came from a wealthy family of Argentine-Portuguese origin. He enjoyed the quiet happy childhood, and the careful education, under strong Church influence, usually received by the children of well-to-do families in Chile of that day.

In 1849 he was placed in the Colegio run by a French order in Santiago, and in 1852 entered the Seminario Conciliar in the same city, to prepare for the priesthood. He was a bright student, and in his seminary days he showed a strong tendency toward mysticism—not unusual in his day and age. Among his first writings, dating from his student years, is a highly mystic eulogy of the Archbishop of Santiago.

Yet evidently his devotion to the priesthood was not entirely a settled matter, for in 1864 he welcomed the opportunity to accompany ex-president Manuel Montt, now Chief Justice of the Supreme Court, on a mission to Lima in connection with the war of Chile and Peru against Spain. This contact with his father's friend, Montt, the influence of a younger colleague of the mission, Zentano, and the acquaintance with diplomatic society in Lima seem to have had the effect of converting Balmaceda to the cause of liberal reform at this time. At all events, he had given up the idea of a clerical career by the time he returned to Chile.

He undertook the management of two haciendas belonging to his father, Peralillo and Lipangui, and soon married Emilia de Toro Herrera, the daughter of another Chilean family of wealth and position. The spirit of liberal reform was growing in Chile in the 1860's. The election of President Pérez in 1861 represented a partial concession to this new tendency on the part of the long dominant conservative party. Balmaceda's conversion to this movement of reform and his rising political ambitions soon appeared in his collaboration in the founding of a liberal journal, La Libertad, in 1866.

It was almost a foregone conclusion, of course, that a person of his wealth and position would someday enter congress, if he so desired. In

---

[2] Délano, Luis Enrique. Balmaceda, político romántico. Santiago de Chile, Ercilla. 1937. 198p.

September 1858 he joined with a group of other young liberals in organizing the Reform Club (Club de la Reforma). The club consisted of a group of young enthusiasts who were for the most part friends and partisans of ex-President Montt, then Chief Justice, and under severe attack at the time from the administration and congress. The Club was a forum for political debates and speeches demanding reforms, particularly reform of the electoral laws and limitation of the almost dictatorial powers of the president, who, under the Constitution of 1833, could control the election and appointment of officials. From the Reform Club sprang the Liberal Democratic Party, and it was as a candidate of this party that Balmaceda entered congress in 1870, representing the Department of Carelmapu.

As a member of congress he took an active part in the extended debate on constitutional reforms which went on during the early years of the 1870's. One of the proposals much debated during these years was that of limiting the presidency to one term. Some favored a seven-year term with no reelection, but Balmaceda urged, although unsuccessfully, a provision which would have retained the five-year term of the presidency while requiring that ten years elapse before a president might be eligible for reelection. He supported the constitutional reforms, adopted in 1874, which limited the presidency to one five-year term; prohibited members of parliament from holding any other remunerative position under the government except that of minister; provided for the direct election of senators; limited the extraordinary powers which might be granted to the president by congress; changed the method of selection of the Comisión Conservadora, which acted for congress while it was not in session; restricted the president's control over the courts; extended congressional control over the Council of State; and limited the authority of the administration to intervene in the conduct of elections.

Balmaceda also gave enthusiastic support to other measures favored by the liberals of his day. He urged government financial aid for the construction of railroads and educational missions for the Araucanian Indians. He urged reforms in the criminal laws, such as abolition of whipping and of the death penalty. He fought against continuance of the tobacco monopoly, which was not abolished, however, until 1880. But especially, during these years in congress, he concentrated upon urging electoral and constitutional reforms, becoming one of the nation's leading spokesmen for a more democratic and freer system of elections.

By the time of the presidential election of 1881 Balmaceda had become a political leader of national prominence in the Liberal Democratic Party. During the term of President Pinto, just ending, the administration had relied considerably upon the support of the various Liberal parties in congress, even though nominal leadership was in the hands of the Nationalist Party. Like other liberals, Balmaceda had supported the Pinto administration in its program of Church reforms, including the establishment of civil marriage and civil registration of births and deaths—reforms which involved the government in a serious dispute with high officials of the Church in Chile. He and his friends played a large part in the election of President Santa María in 1881. Santa María enjoyed the support of President Pinto. It is not entirely clear just what Balmaceda's role was in this election since his biographers have not studied the question carefully. It is evident, however, that he must have played an important part, since he became a member of the Santa María cabinet. The one thing which appears most clearly is that he persuaded his personal friend, General Baquedano, a Liberal candidate and hero of the War of the Pacific, to withdraw his candidacy in favor of Santa María, with the result that Santa María was elected without any formal opposition.

Meanwhile, Balmaceda had taken an active part in two matters affecting the international relations of his country. On the eve of the War of the Pacific he was sent on a special diplomatic mission to Argentina, where he succeeded in postponing a serious boundary controversy with that country, thus keeping Argentina neutral during the war. Later, as Minister of Foreign Affairs, he was to negotiate an agreement with Argentina for settlement of this boundary by arbitration. His attitude during the War of the Pacific may justly be described as chauvinistic. He was already coming to think of himself as the tribune of the masses and during the war indulged in especially violent and passionate appeals to his countrymen to pursue the war against Peru and Bolivia relentlessly. This same national spirit led him to help thwart the Blaine-Garfield plan for a Pan-American Conference. His colleague and apologist, Bañados Espinosa, inaccurately claims that he prevented United States intervention in the War of the Pacific at this time. This is clearly an exaggeration, but there is little doubt that Balmaceda had become the spokesman of a new spirit of national self-confidence in Chile which was to have a great influence not only upon the next two decades of that nation's history but upon his own subsequent political career as well.

As Minister of the Interior in the Santa María cabinet, Balmaceda was presumably the favored or "official" candidate for the presidency. Normally this would have meant support of the National Party and various liberal groups, including the Liberal Democratic Party. As the time of the presidential election drew near, however, a strange situation developed in Chilean party politics. No party could claim a majority in the congress. The two parties of greatest influence, the Conservative Party and the Nationalist Party (the party of Manuel Montt) were the nuclei of the fundamental political grouping, but both represented the old oligarchy and felt the need for support of the various liberal groups which represented the new, more popular and democratic forces. President Santa María had tried to bring Nationalists and the various factions among the Liberals and Radicals to give united support to Balmaceda's candidacy, but had not been successful in doing so. One faction of the Liberals and one faction of the Radicals joined the conservatives in opposition. However, as in the congressional elections of 1882, they stayed away from the polls, so that Balmaceda was elected without opposition.

The party disputes in congress during the last months of the Santa María administration had been particularly bitter, presaging the lines of division of the revolution of five years later. The opposition (conservative) minority resorted to every device of parliamentary obstructionism to prevent the enactment of an appropriations bill, a tactic designed to force the government to resort to extraordinary (dictatorial) powers to carry on the functions of government. In this purpose they succeeded with help of Liberals, and the Balmaceda regime began in an atmosphere of tension which augured ill for its success. Joaquim Nabuco has observed that the parties who pursued these dilatory tactics in 1886 were in part the very ones who rushed to arms in 1891 to assert the authority of congress over the president.

President Balmaceda was overthrown in 1891 by a revolution which grew out of a constitutional controversy. But behind the constitutional controversy lay the program of social and economic reforms of his administration. As a member of the Santa María cabinet, as noted, he had helped carry through the program of clerical reforms, yet one of his first acts as president was to resume relations with the Vatican under a *modus vivendi*. Some of the bitterness of the dispute was thus alleviated, but conservative clerical leaders were not conciliated—they were in fact further antagonized and alienated by his economic policies.

By 1887 the national revenue had grown to three times that of a decade earlier, reflecting a great growth in national income, especially income derived from foreign trade. Balmaceda urged a program of national expenditures and activities in proportion, while conservatives felt the increased revenue would be better used to reduce the national debt. The Balmaceda government inaugurated one thousand miles of railroad construction, as much as had been undertaken under all previous governments. Several thousand kilometers of new highways were opened, and bridges and harbors were built. A subsidy was granted for completion of the Trans-Andean Railway through the Uspallata Pass. Telephone service was inaugurated between Valparaiso and Santiago, and three thousand miles of telegraph lines were built. A complete naval reorganization was carried out and several new cruisers built. Great progress was made in education, and sixty large primary schools were built by the nationalist government, as well as three normal schools and a building to house the national office of education. The objective of the educational program was a school in every village. Balmaceda's restless reforming energy turned also to prison reform, and brought about a reorganization of the prison system. Twenty new hospitals were also built.

Among the reforms urged by the president, one which aroused great apprehension among his conservative opponents was the proposal for the election of the president by popular vote. He was also supposedly hostile to the interests of foreign capital, and British diplomatic correspondence of the day reflects a generally hostile attitude towards the Balmaceda government. But above all, the conservative oligarchy in Chile, entrenched in the conservative and liberal parties, feared this new popular appeal to the lower classes, feared Balmaceda's growing popularity with the workers, and saw in his rule the forecast of the end of their long domination of national political life.

As the time for the next presidential election drew near, congress, long hostile to Balmaceda's reforms and to his ambitious program of public works, tried to block his plans for nominating his successor. His wish was to nominate his Minister of the Interior, Enrique Sanfuentes. When a vote of censure failed to bring resignation of the cabinet, congress resorted to refusing to vote appropriations. Balmaceda then appeared to yield, allowing Sanfuentes to resign, and congress voted a temporary appropriation to the new cabinet under Belisario Prats. Congress and cabinet then began removing intendants and other officials through whom it was felt the president might control the elections.

Congress then adjourned, still without voting a regular appropriations bill, and the president recalled them in special session. When they still remained adamant, he dismissed the Prats cabinet and prorogued congress, appointing a new and friendly cabinet. At this point the Comisión Conservadora, a body which was authorized to act for the congress when it was not in session, stepped in, advising a new session of congress, and when Balmaceda refused to take this step, issued the call in its own name—an act of doubtful constitutionality.

The deadlock between the president and a congress of dubious legal standing continued. Appropriations expired on January 1, 1891, and the president, speaking again in accordance with his concept of the president as a tribune of the people, issued a manifesto saying he would run the government, if necessary, without congress. He could not recognize, he said, the validity of principles of parliamentary government when these principles were not in the constitution.

The Liberal Party, which had risen to such great influence since the middle of the nineteenth century, had accomplished its main purposes in reforms which stripped the Church of many of its prerogatives and in constitutional reforms which reduced the extraordinary powers which the president enjoyed under the Constitution of 1833. His power to declare a state of siege had been restricted, his veto power had been limited, his control over elections had been restrained by increasing local controls, even his control over his cabinet had been affected by congressional assertion of the right to interpellate ministers and even to force their resignation by a formal vote of censure. With the passing of the years, and especially after the increased prosperity which followed the War of the Pacific, the Liberal Party became increasingly conservative, and, what was even more fatal, broke up into several factions. One of these factions, including the more radical advocates of constitutional reforms, such as parliamentary government, had formed the Radical Party.

During the first years of his presidency Balmaceda had successfully united the various Liberal parties, but in the struggle which ensued the conservatives had managed to turn most of the Liberals against him. Subsequent events proved rather clearly that the president's effort to oppose the oligarchy in the selection of his successor, and his dictatorial attempt to govern without congress were serious mistakes. More than that, they were unconstitutional acts which could not be tolerated in Chile. But the struggle between president and congress was not the real issue. Behind the constitutional conflict lay the threat of Balmaceda's appeal to the new sources of social discontent in Chile, especially the urban workers who now enjoyed the suffrage. The president's effort to restore his office to the powerful position it had enjoyed half a century before, and especially his proposal for the popular election of presidents, thus seemed to strike at the very roots of the power of the oligarchy which had ruled Chile for sixty years, whether the President happened to be a conservative, a liberal or a nationalist.

On the very day of Balmaceda's proclamation a rump congress declared the president deposed and placed the navy under the command of Captain Jorge Montt, son of the ex-president. The president declared martial law and civil war was on. In the main the navy sided with the congressional party, while the army remained loyal to Balmaceda. Yet even here the class basis of the struggle appeared in the fact that the army was lacking in capable and trained officers. Many of the most able officers had been removed or transferred to inactive assignments because of suspected disloyalty. The congressionalists siezed Iquique, the nitrate port in the north, but seemed unable to undertake any large-scale land operations. The Balmacedistas, on the other hand, were unable to take positive steps to suppress the rebellion because they were lacking in naval support. For a long time they were blocked in their efforts to get the French courts to release two new cruisers under construction in France, which would have materially strengthened their position.

Meanwhile, in the south, the government proceeded with elections. A congress favorable to Balmaceda was elected and at once legalized all presidential acts since January 1, 1891. Discussion of various constitutional reforms began immediately. Soon, in the presidential elections, a majority of electors was returned favorable to Claudio Vicuña, the candidate supported by Balmaceda.

At this point, before the presidential election could be officially consumated, the rebels began their long waited invasion at Valparaiso. Government forces suffered two severe defeats, at Concón and at Las Cadenas, and the congressional forces soon occupied the capital.

Balmaceda took refuge in the Argentine embassy. There, a few days later, after learning of the persecutions being visited upon his followers, he committed suicide, apparently in the hope that his death might lessen the bitterness toward his political friends.

Out of this constitutional struggle came a political revolution which brought parliamentary-cabinet government to Chile in 1891. It was ironical that this change, giving political supremacy to the representatives of the people in congress, a liberal reform, had been carried out in Chile by representatives of a conservative political and social oligarchy.[3] The system was to continue unchallenged, until Arturo Alessandri appeared in the 1920's to combat the power of this political oligarchy in the name of long overdue social and economic reform.

Balmaceda's romantic suicide was the tragic end of a phase of the movement for democratic reform in Chile. Yet it was only a temporary defeat, because of his resort to a presidential dictatorship. His followers, now known as *Balmacedistas*, soon formed the Democratic Party, and under the leadership of Enrique Sanfuentes, renewed the campaign for reform. The example which he had set was a powerful one, and as far away as Uruguay aspiring young political idealists like Baltazaar Brum saw that the constitutional questions involved in the struggle in Chile were not the real issues, and that Balmaceda's real significance lay in his bold challenge of the power of the political oligarchy which opposed social and economic reform. Thirty-five years later the forces of reform, under Arturo Alessandri, justified Balmaceda in at least one respect. As part of their program of reform, they greatly modified the parliamentary system by increasing the powers of the president to control his cabinet and the intendants of the provinces, and provided for the direct election of the president for a single six-year term.

Délano, Luis Enrique. Balmaceda, político romántico. Santiago de Chile, Ercilla. 1937. 198p.

Nabuco, Joaquim. Balmaceda. São Paulo, Companhia Editora Nacional and Rio de Janeiro, Civilização Brasileira, S. A. 1937. 200p. (Published originally as a series of articles in the Jornal de Comercio in 1895, and as a book in the same year in Rio de Janeiro and in Val-

[3] See J. Fred Rippy, *Historical Evolution of Hispanic America*. New York, F. S. Crofts. 2d ed. 1940. p248.

paraiso in Spanish translation. This work is a criticism of a book by
Julio Bañados Espinosa: Balmaceda, su gobierno y la revolución de
1891, published in 1894.)

Salas Edwards, Ricardo. Balmaceda y el parlamentarismo en Chile. 2d ed.
Santiago de Chile, Sociedad Imprenta y Litografía Universo. 1916.

United States Congress. Message of the President transmitting the correspondence between the United States and Chile. (52d Congress, 1st
session. House Executive Documents, v34, no. 91) Washington, D.C.,
Government Printing Office. 1892. p90ff.

Wilgus, A. Curtis, ed. South American dictators during the first century
of independence. (Studies in Hispanic American Affairs, v5) Washington, D.C., George Washington University Press. 1937. p198-211.
Balmaceda, liberal dictator of Chile. L. W. Bealer.

Yrarrázaval Larrain, José Miguel. El presidente Balmaceda. Santiago de
Chile, Nascimento. 1940. 2v. 466, 396p. (An excellent review of
this book, by Maury Austin Bromsen, appeared in Hispanic American
Historical Review. 22:113-16. February 1942.)

HIPÓLITO IRIGOYEN (1852-1933)

THE ARGENTINE MAN OF MYSTERY

Time must still elapse before history can render an objective verdict on the career of the founder and leader of the Argentine Radical Party. Elected with great popular acclaim to the presidency in 1916, at the culmination of a long crusade for political reform, he led his country through the troubled neutrality of World War I and managed at the same time to achieve part at least of the domestic reforms promised by his party. Reelected in 1928, at the age of seventy-six, to serve another term, he appeared unable to deal with the national problems presented by the collapse in world trade and the consequent disruption of Argentine economic life, so closely tied to world trade. What can only be described as a great silence followed. The great commoner of Argentina sat silent in the Casa Rosada while grave national problems went unsolved, and his party fell to pieces around him. His overthrow by a bloodless revolution in 1930 was doubtless due in large measure to the effects in Argentina of the collapse of world trade. But it marked an epoch in Argentine history—the end of the period of Radical Party rule, and the beginning of the political tendencies which govern Argentina today.

Irigoyen is difficult to classify as a political leader. The Argentine Manuel Gálvez, who has given us the best literary portrait of the man, urges an analogy to the political career of Juan Manuel Rosas, the sinister dictator of early Argentine history, an analogy which hardly seems justified. There are numerous resemblances, to be sure, but they are more superficial than real. The political power of both was based on the province of Buenos Aires and upon a great popular following among the disinherited among the Porteños; and both were in a peculiar fashion the product of the Argentine political and social environment. But while Rosas' objectives were power and the maintenance of order, Irigoyen set out to demonstrate that the Argentine masses were capable of democratic self-government. He is more like an Andrew Jackson, a William Jennings Bryan, or a Francisco Madero in this democratic apostolate. Paradoxically he was the first Argentine leader to demonstrate the effectiveness of mass national party organization, and did not hesitate during his long and troubled political career to make use of practices suggestive of the political "boss." In this and the development of popular national party organization and activity, his career suggests that of Jackson.

Yet there are subtle and elusive facets in his political activity which are typically Argentine. Chiefly it showed a spirit of bravado, which was, perhaps, *gaucho* or creole in character. It was this spirit which led him to act by organizing, or threatening to organize, revolutions—because the Argentine political mind respected such demonstrations of strength and courage. At the same time, however, he worked with the greatest care to give these uprisings an organized popular form, which made them chiefly demonstrations of the force and power of the party; and he tried meticulously to avoid bloodshed. Organizer of popular revolutions, he was a pacifist with almost a mania for avoiding bloodshed, and even in 1930, when the employment of military force might conceivably have prevented his overthrow, he refused to give his approval to a course of action which would lead to violence.

He was one of the most powerful leaders in the history of Argentine politics, and his influence was uniquely personal. He exercised great attraction over his followers, and he built the Radical Party, to a large extent, on loyalty to himself. In 1930 his party split on the grounds of his dominance, the *anti-personalistas* supporting the revolutionary opposition. Yet he himself had given much of his political career to an apostolic campaign against "personalism" in the oligarchy which controlled Argentina at the end of the nineteenth century. His own loyalty was to reform and to what he called the cultivation of civic virtue, and from the time of his withdrawal from the national legislature in 1890 until his election to the presidency in 1916, he consistently refused all political offices offered to him. He accepted the presidential nomination in 1916 only when the party leaders threatened to dissolve the party unless he accepted.

Irigoyen was born in Buenos Aires on July 12, 1852, the year of the fall of the dictator Rosas. His father was a poor French Basque immigrant, Martín Irigoyen Dodagaray, and his mother, Marcelina Alén, was the daughter of Leandro Alén, who was executed the following year for his alleged crimes as a vigilante of the Rosas government. Hipólito thus grew up in an atmosphere of fear in a family which had been closely associated with Rosas, and constantly felt that it was being spied on. His maternal uncle, Leandro Alem (or Alén) fought with Urquiza a few years later at the battles of Cepeda (1859) and Pavón (1861). Yet the shadow of his executed grandfather still hung over young Hipólito when, at the age of ten, he and his brother entered the Colegio de San José. A strangely silent boy, who seldom took part in games, he was frequently taunted by the other boys for being the grandson of the hanged man.

In school he was serious and studious. Although never the highest in his class, he was always to be seen with books under his arm. Later he entered the Colegio de América, founded by a Spanish clergyman who was the lover of his aunt—a school in which his Uncle Leandro was now an instructor. His education was irregular. During the Paraguayan War, as a boy of thirteen or fourteen, he found various employments while his uncle was serving with the army. At the age of sixteen or seventeen he worked for a while in a law office. When he was seventeen he secured a clerical position in the government with the help of his uncle who had now returned from the army and from a diplomatic mission to Brazil. At the age of twenty, he was named commissioner of police for his ward, Balvanera, also through Leandro's influence. Leandro had become the political boss of this turbulent district of the city, in whose very air one breathed politics, and Hipólito was not long in learning the ways of the ward boss, nor in demonstrating his ability to control men. In 1873 he and his uncle supported Alsina and his Autonomous Party in opposition to Mitre's National Party, in the provincial elections. Alsina, as governor of Buenos Aires, had led the fight against federalizing the city of Buenos Aires. He was a *compadre* of Balvanera, the *caudillo* type, and had a strong following among old *Rosistas* and federalists, including Negroes of the ward.

In spite of his youth Irigoyen was successful as police commissioner, and held the office until 1877, when he was removed by political enemies of his uncle for his part in disturbances in the ward during an electoral campaign. Meanwhile, he had secured special permission to enter the University and had pursued a course in law. Whether or not he completed the course three years later has been the subject of some argument. There are irregularities in the University records and some of the records of his work are missing. But he used the title of Doctor thereafter and the probability is that he received a degree in regular course at this time.

About this time, too, when he was twenty-five, he fell in love with Domingo Campos, daughter of a distinguished family in the city. His financial insecurity, and possibly the opposition of her family prevented marriage. But for twelve years, until her death in 1889 from pulmonary tuberculosis, he was her devoted, if not always faithful, lover. Several children were born to them, and Irigoyen was at the point of marrying her at the time of her death. He never married, as a matter of fact. Women were always greatly attracted to him and he had a series of love affairs— not an unusual occurrence in his day in Argentina. The unusual thing was that he never spoke of these affairs, and they would have gone unnoticed if his enemies had not tried to make political capital out of his natural children.

The action of Hipólito and his uncle in the election of 1873 has already been noted. Leandro Alem was elected national deputy at this time, and soon became increasingly important as the leader of reform tendencies in Argentina. Irigoyen's removal from the office of police commissioner in 1877 proved to be just the beginning of a more active political career. The next year he was elected a provincial deputy with the support of his uncle, Del Valle, and the Republican Party. By this time he had become an important political lieutenant of his uncle, and his purpose in entering the legislature was to oppose federalizing the city of Buenos Aires. Uncle and nephew broke with Del Valle on this account, when the latter led his party back into the Autonomous Party in cooperation with the former President Bartolomé Mitre. As the election of 1880 approached, however, they also entered the Autonomous Party, but only after the latter party had separated from Mitre and his followers.

The years from 1878 to 1880 were turbulent years in Argentine politics and in Irigoyen's life. He distinguished himself as an able leader in the provincial legislature. After the excitement attending the election of General Julio Roca as president in 1880 he supported President Nicolás Avellaneda in the conflict with Governor Carlos Tejedor of Buenos Aires, and accompanied the president to Belgrano when he was forced to leave the capital. The defeat of Tejedor paved the way for the federalization of the national capital, and Irigoyen entered the national congress as an *Autonomista*.

He was soon in opposition to President Roca. Increasing immigration and the rapid growth of urban population were introducing a new element of political unrest into Argentine life. Under the administration of Roca the trend toward oligarchical control, which tended toward more and more restriction of the suffrage, and to the selection of provincial governors and even legislatures by the oligarchy, became increasingly marked. Leandro Alem became the popular leader of opposition to these tendencies and Irigoyen followed his lead. After less than two years in the national congress, however, he withdrew to live for a decade in relative political obscurity. He had been named professor of history and philosophy in the Escuela Normal de Maestras in 1880, and now divided his time between his professorial duties, in which he was highly successful, and the improvement of two farms, Santa María and Santa Isabel, which he bought at this time with money borrowed from the Bank of the Province. Here he engaged in a profitable business of buying and fattening cattle for the market —a business which gave him, if not wealth, at least financial competence from this time on.

This period of withdrawal from active politics had a profound influence on his life. In some way he became a "convert" to Krausism, the "spiritual" philosophy which was then gaining great popularity in the Spanish speaking world. The philosophy of Kraus became a religion to him— a religion of humanity and human equality, of pacifism, and of human welfare. It led to an interest in social questions such as the welfare of workers, to an emphasis upon the moral and spiritual aspects of all questions, and to considering reason as immanent in all things. Irigoyen gave his professorial salary to the Sociedad de Beneficencia, thus acquiring a reputation for philanthropy although he was not a rich man. Later he was to do the same with his presidential salary. Except for his relations with women, he lived a life of great social austerity, never going to dances or to the theatre, and was seldom seen at social gatherings of any kind. He accepted no offices, and in his single room in the house of Leandro Alem, lived almost the life of a monk.

The year 1890 marked his return to active politics. In that year he took part, with Del Valle and Leandro Alem, in the uprising which overthrew President Juárez Celman. When, however, Del Valle proposed endorsing Mitre as the presidential candidate of the revolutionary party, Irigoyen, almost alone, spoke out against it and in favor of a national convention of the party to select a candidate. The national convention was held—the first in Argentina. Irigoyen, knowing he would fail to defeat the selection of Mitre, characteristically refused to attend the convention.

It was during the next decade that this inveterate political conspirator showed his true political genius in forging the Unión Cívica Radical (Radical Party) out of a series of apparent political defeats. In 1892 he organized the party in the province of Buenos Aires, and thereafter his control of this overwhelmingly powerful province was the mainstay of his political influence. The effectiveness of his political organization of the province appeared in the bloodless revolution of 1893, which overthrew the provincial government almost overnight. It was a demonstration of uncanny political sagacity and dissimulation, carried out almost entirely by word of mouth, without writing or proclamations. Irigoyen became the head of a group of youthful leaders in the party which eventually drove out the older leaders, including his uncle, Leandro Alem, who soon renounced leadership of the party. When Alem committed suicide political enemies were not lacking to charge that Irigoyen's pitiless opposition was responsible for this family tragedy.

The strength of his party was built on undeviating opposition to transactions with any other political groups, and to its consistent demand for electoral reform. Such political intransigence was practically unknown in Argentina, and the leaders of the old parties scarcely knew how to deal with it. In 1894 Irigoyen refused to sanction an agreement with the followers of Mitre (Unión Cívica Nacional) which would have made possible their joint triumph in electing a governor in Buenos Aires. A few months later he refused a nomination as national senator on the same grounds. In 1898 he refused to make an agreement with the Mitristas to prevent the reelection of President Roca, and refused a nomination for the governorship of Buenos Aires.

The Radicals refrained from voting in the election of 1904. In protest against continuation of the "oligarchical" system under President Manuel Quintana, in that year, they also carried out a widespread national uprising, with the support of a considerable part of the army. In the course of this uprising it became clear that Irigoyen's great gift for political organization and conspiracy was not matched by the qualities of decisive action as a revolutionary leader. Either because of his lack of ability to act decisively at the right time, or because of fundamental opposition to forcing a decision by arms, he missed several opportunities to make the revolution a success and it was quickly suppressed by vigorous government action. The upshot was that the uprising seemed to have been chiefly a widespread civic demonstration of the strength of the Radical Party, and of the strength of their demand for electoral reform. Thus, strangely, as the years went by, this "unsuccessful" revolution proved to be one of the greatest political assets of the party. The electoral reform which they demanded was soon accomplished by a new law passed in 1912, during the presidency of Roque Sáenz Peña. The Radical Party then reentered active political life, and Irigoyen was elected president in 1916.

His record as president from 1916 to 1922 is one of the most controversial in Argentina's history. He had immense personal prestige and great power over the Radical Party which clearly commanded a majority in the country. But powerful influences opposed him and he had almost constant difficulty with congress. The avowed friend of the masses and of organized labor, he succeeded in securing the passage of various social reform measures, including a minimum wage law. Yet he called out the army to suppress a strike of stevedores in Buenos Aires, with great resulting loss of lives. This action cost him much of his previous popularity in labor circles. In keeping Argentina neutral during World War I, likewise, he showed little regard for powerful public opinion which demanded support of the Allies in the war.

He was succeeded by another radical, Marcelo T. Alvear (1922-1928), who encountered serious difficulty in a struggle over a workmen's compensation act, in a quarrel with the Church, and in relations with the United States. Irigoyen was reelected in 1928, in a great demonstration of personal popularity, only to be driven from office in 1930. During this second term he was aging and seemed somehow to have lost his former influence over many of his followers. One faction of the Radical party, the anti-personalists, had, in fact, openly opposed his reelection. Isolated from the public and from party leaders by a small coterie of his followers, he neglected many pressing matters growing out of the world financial crisis and trade breakdown, treated departmental heads in an autocratic, highhanded manner, and intervened in provincial affairs in a way which brought much criticism. Industrial unrest and continuance of the depression caused him to lose much of his former popularity. Outwardly, at least, his administration seemed to have reached a state of complete paralysis bcause of the president's isolation from party leaders and his insistence that everything pass through his hands.

On September 6, 1930 he was overthrown by a military uprising, supported by a combination of conservatives, anti-personalist radicals, and sc cialists. The opposition of the socialists meant that he had lost much of the support of organized labor groups through failure to take adequate measures to deal with the economic crisis. Yet the combination of parties which overthrew him apparently could not muster a popular majority and had to resort to controlled elections two years later to secure the election of a president. By vigorous measures the revolt could probably have been suppressed. Irigoyen may have been overly confident in the strength of his popular support, trusting too much the kind of political clairvoyance which had stood him in good stead throughout his career and which now led him to feel that the revolution would not succeed. For some reason he refused to believe those who told him how serious the situation had become. Or it may have been his old reluctance to employ force in what he considered a political contest which caused him to hesitate to take the vigorous military measures necessary to suppress the rebellion.

General José Evaristo Uriburu, leader of the revolt, occupied Buenos Aires with what was a very small force indeed. Irigoyen was imprisoned for about two years. Released, he lived quietly for six months in Buenos Aires until his death in 1933. The popular demonstrations in the city following his death rivaled or even exceeded those which had been accorded Bartolomé Mitre. He had always conducted politics with an air of mystery, and this same air of mystery hung over the end of his career. He left few papers which throw any light on the great tragedy of his political life— the revolution of 1930, from which so much of the present political situation in Argentina is derived. Nor is there any record to explain the great public demonstration at his death, a demonstration which provided such a striking contrast to his apparently complete loss of public affection three years before.

Current History. 30:869-75. August 1929. President Irigoyen of Argentina. Hugo Wast (Gustavo Martínez Zuviría).

Current History. 38:728-9. September 1933. Passing of Irigoyen. H. G. Doyle.

Gálvez, Manuel. Vida de Hipólito Yrigoyen. 2d ed. Buenos Aires, The Author. 1939. 476p.

Marcosson, I. F. Turbulent years. New York, Dodd, Mead. 1938. p279-315.

Nation. 128:70-1. January 16, 1929. President Irigoyen of Argentina. P. V. Shaw.

Rodríguez Yrigoyen, Luis. Hipólito Yrigoyen, 1878-1933. Buenos Aires, The Author. 1934. 534p. (Collection of documents)

Saturday Evening Post. 204:16-17. January 16, 1932. Argentine advance. I. F. Marcosson.

World's Work. 59:88-91. March 1930. Mystery man of Argentina. T. R. Ybarra.

RUY BARBOSA (1849-1923)

BRAZILIAN LIBERAL

Most Brazilians, whatever their political views, take pride in Ruy Barbosa as a great scholar, reformer, and crusader for civil liberties. His international importance was recently recognized anew in the publication in Mexico of an imposing work, consisting of excerpts from his political writings, in the series *El pensamiento de América*. A diplomatic representative of the United States in Brazil has also recently honored him by publishing his biography in English.[1]

Barbosa was one of the great intellectuals of his day in Brazil. He was most at home in his forty-thousand-volume library of English, French, German, Italian, Spanish, and Portuguese books. (His library was uncatalogued, for he said he knew where every book was.) An accomplished linguist, he spoke fluently in English, Italian, French, and Spanish. Moreover, he looked the part of a scholar. He was small and slender in build —hardly the appearance expected of a crusading political leader. When he spoke, however, one was immediately impressed with his rich, sonorous voice, and began to get some idea of the secret of his capacity to charm and win people with his oratory. He is remembered today for his vehement pleas for the abolition of slavery, for his bold defense of the victims of dictatorship, and for his valiant and successful campaign against militarism in Brazilian politics, especially in the election of 1910. He represents the power of the spoken and written word, for it was his speeches and writing which made him a force in Brazilian politics. They were also a rich contribution to the literature and thought of Brazil. Haunting phrases of Ruy Barbosa still find echoes in Brazilian political discussion.

His capacity for work was enormous, and this, more even than his intellectual and oratorical abilities, accounts for his achievements. He held numerous political offices, although this part of his career might not seem outstanding. He was a member of the imperial assembly for several years; he was minister of finance and justice in the provisional government established at the time of the overthrow of the monarchy in 1889; he was a member of the senate under the republic; he represented Brazil at the Second Hague Conference in 1907; and he conducted one of the most vigorous popular campaigns for the Brazilian presidency in 1910 which the country had ever seen. But his greatest success in politics was of another character, as already suggested. It lay in winning men and parties to his views on

[1] Turner, Charles William. *Ruy Barbosa, Brazilian Crusader for the Essential Freedoms.* Nashville, Tenn., Abingdon-Cokesbury. 1945. 208p.

human slavery, political corruption, militarism, and dictatorship in politics
—in a lifelong campaign for democracy and for constitutional government.

He was born November 5, 1849, in São Salvador (Bahia), in north-
eastern Brazil, the second child of João José Barbosa and María Adelia.
His name, Ruy, a diminutive of Rodrigo, was a common name in the Barbosa family. His father was a physician of modest means and accomplishments, who distinguished himself in Bahian politics as a liberal leader in
the days of the empire, as a deputy in the provincial assembly, and as the
director of public education. In this latter capacity he reformed the school
system of the province. He was also—and this was important in forming
the ideas of his son—an ardent admirer of the political institutions of Britain
and the United States.

Ruy's first teacher was Antonio Gentil Ibirapitanga, who claimed afterwards that he had taught Ruy to read in fifteen days, and that in thirty
years' teaching he had never seen anything to equal the boy's speed in
learning. He was clearly a superior student. In the Ginásio Bahiano, where
he studied the humanities with Abilio Cesar Borges, later Baron of Maca-
hubas, he won the school's gold medal for scholarship. Here, also, he
studied mathematics with the gifted but eccentric Silva Pereira, who was
known throughout the country for his short temper and acid tongue.

At the age of seventeen Barbosa entered the law school at Recife.
Later he studied at the University of São Paulo, from which he was grad-
uated in 1870. There, as a university student, he began his career as an
orator and crusader for liberal causes. He was twenty years old when he
gave his first public address in São Paulo on the subject "The Servile Element." It was an argument against slavery on the grounds that it was
inferior economically to free labor, that it hindered immigration, that it was
morally wrong, and that it was in large measure illegal, since many of the
slaves had been brought into the country in violation of the law of 1831
which outlawed the slave trade. This speech won him considerable renown
among the students, and he soon became known as a liberal but "noisy"
speaker. From the members of his Masonic lodge, consisting largely of
sons of wealthy *fazendeiros,* he secured a pledge to free the offspring of
their slaves.

. At this time, too, Barbosa became a friend of Castro Alves, the great
Brazilian poet of Negro life, who died a few years later, and of Joaquim
Nabuco, destined to become one of Brazil's outstanding statesmen. The
Paraguayan War was then drawing to a close, and Ruy, like many other
students in São Paulo, was aroused to protest against the order to hunt down
and kill the fugitive Paraguayan president-dictator, Solano López. He and
his friends made it clear that they did not defend the cause of the dictator,
but were protesting against the inhumanity of the man hunt. Naturally
their stand aroused great feeling, and added to Ruy's reputation as a "radi-

cal." About this time, also, he and Americo de Campos founded a journal, *O radical paulistano*, which the youthful editors proclaimed to profess "liberal tenets in all their fullness."

After finishing his law course he stayed in São Paulo for several years, until his father's death in 1874 recalled him to Bahia. His father had left many debts which Ruy courageously undertook to repay. Soon he was associated with all his father's liberal political friends. He became editor of the *Diario da Bahia*, and from its pages led a vigorous anti-slavery crusade.

At this point it may be well to note the history of Negro emancipation in Brazil and its relation to the other forces and tendencies which brought about the overthrow of the empire and the establishment of a republic in 1889. Society in Brazil was highly stratified, so that political influence was in the hands of a relatively small part of the population, predominantly the *fazendeiros*, or owners of estates, who held the important positions in government, in the army and in the Church. The empire rested upon the support of this *fazendeiro* class, upon the support of the Church, and upon the army. Since the Paraguayan War (1864-70) the prestige of the army had greatly increased, and its political support was accordingly greater.

Trouble with the Church came when the government prosecuted two bishops in 1873 for unlawfully publishing the Papal Syllabus for the Episcopate of 1864, and for initiating a campaign against the Freemasons. Although the Papacy supported the government, the latter lost much of its previous support among the clergy. The effort in 1883 to prevent army officers from taking an active part in politics was even more costly, and the government had to back down when the army cause was taken up by General Manoel Deodoro da Fonseca, later military leader of the revolution, and first president of the republic. Lack of popular confidence in the emperor's only remaining child, Isabella, and her French husband, Gaston d'Orléans, son of Louis Philippe of France, also cost the empire in prestige.

It was the slavery issue, however, which finally brought on a revolution which replaced the Brazilian empire with a republican government. After more than twenty years of agitation the slave trade was finally abolished by a law of 1853. Meanwhile abolitionist sentiment grew rapidly, although opposed in general by the conservatives. Brazil helped bring about emancipation in Paraguay at the end of the Paraguayan War, and shortly afterward the Rio Branco Law was passed (1871), providing that all children of slave parents born after that date should be free. Voluntary emancipation was frequent, and in 1884 the provinces of Ceará and Amazonas freed their slaves. The next year, after a bitter political struggle, an imperial law was enacted liberating all slaves over sixty. The chief opposition to these measures centered in the land- and slave-owning class which wanted compensation.

Meanwhile the constant talk of emancipation and the agitation of abolitionists were responsible for a great increase in the number of runaway
slaves, so that it began to look as though the whole system of property in
slaves might simply disintegrate. When the army was called to assist in
returning the fugitives, army officers protested and the plan was abandoned.
The Princess Isabella, acting as regent in her father's absence, thus had to
face a new crisis in the slavery issue. She was an ardent abolitionist herself
and determined to end the crisis by securing passage of a law of immediate
emancipation. As a result of her insistence an emancipation bill was introduced into the Chamber of Deputies, where it received the enthusiastic support of Joaquim Nabuco. Passed by both houses it became law in May
1888. This measure, as Isabella's ministers had advised her, cost the empire
the support of the conservatives. Nor was a short-lived liberal ministry
which followed any more successful in unifying the nation, even though it
undertook a number of reforms and tried to arrange for some kind of compensation for the freed slaves. It was the deathblow to the empire, and it
was only a few months until a bloodless revolution occurred, led by Benjamin Constant and by Generals Manoel Deodoro da Fonseca and Floriano
Peixoto. Ruy Barbosa's role in this uprising will be noted later.

Two important events marked the year 1877 in Ruy's life. He married
Augusta Vianna Bandeira, and he published his translation of *O Papa e o
Concilio*.² Marriage proved to be the basis of an unusually happy and successful family life. The preface to his translation of *The Pope and the
Council* was one of his greatest works. In it he analyzed the essential place
of religion in all human life, and protested with the strongest religious feeling against the principle of Papal Infallibility, as did the authors of the
work. Twelve years later, under the provisional republic, he was to have
the opportunity to carry out some of the ideas expressed in his preface in a
decree separating Church and State.

On the tenth anniversary (1881) of the death of the poet Castro Alves,
his friend of university days, Barbosa published a eulogy in the form of an
eloquent plea for the emancipation of the people of whom Alves had written
so movingly. That same year he was elected a deputy to the imperial assembly from Bahia.

In the assembly his career was short. One is reminded of Abraham
Lincoln's single term in Congress. Barbosa's assembly career centered
around two issues—education and emancipation. He prepared a report of
the national educational system which won him the title of Counselor of the
Empire. But on the subject of emancipation he was less fortunate. He

² The book published under the pseudonym of Janus was a symposium by Dillinger, Friederich,
and Huber of the University of Munich; Ketteler, Bishop of Mayence; and Maret, Dean of the
Theological Faculty of the Sorbonne. It had been published about a decade earlier, attacking the
doctrine of papal infallibility which had been announced by Pius IX as one of the questions to
be considered at the Council summoned for 1869, the Council from which the Bull of 1870
was derived.

came to the defense of the tottering liberal ministry of Sousa Dantas with an eloquent speech on its project for freeing sexagenarian slaves. And in nineteen days of rapid work he prepared a brilliant report for submission to the assembly, entitled *The Emancipation of the Slaves.* It was a masterly review of the whole subject, but was never officially submitted to the assembly because the ministry fell just at that time. The fall of the ministry was fatal to his immediate political prospects, and he failed of reelection to the assembly. In later years he asserted that the failure of the Sousa Dantas ministry at this time meant the failure of gradual emancipation, and helped bring on the more radical complete abolition by a conservative ministry in 1888, with its inevitable aftermath of the overthrow of the monarchy. Meanwhile, he continued his abolitionist writing and speaking. One of his greatest statements on the subject was his funeral oration for José Bonifacio de Andrada (the younger) in 1886.[3]

For all his sympathy with British and American governments, Barbosa had continued to believe in monarchy, and had not identified himself with republican agitation as represented in the 77 republican newspapers and 273 republican clubs in Brazil, until just before the Revolution of 1889. But he had been carrying on his own vigorous campaign for federalism within the constitutional monarchy. He began the most active phase of this campaign in March 1889, after the issue of slavery was settled, in the *Diario de noticias* of Rio de Janeiro. His attacks in this paper were credited with overthrowing the conservative ministry of João Alfredo Corrêa de Oliveira, in spite of its prestige derived from sponsoring emancipation. In the same manner he helped to overthrow the ministry of the Viscount of Ouro Preto, which was attempting to woo the liberals by financial and economic measures to deal with the dislocations to agriculture resulting from emancipation.

Barbosa was offered a post in the Ouro Preto ministry in accordance with this policy, but he refused to accept unless the ministry would accept his premise of federalism, which it obviously could not do. His attacks in the *Diario de noticias* became even more severe, centering now upon the ministry's policy of distributing the army throughout the provinces to lessen its influence, an influence which had increased greatly since the Paraguayan War. These attacks won him the support of many army leaders, including General Deodoro da Fonseca, and attracted the attention of the positivist Benjamin Constant, professor in the Military College. His federalist campaign thus played a considerable role in the overthrow of the empire, in spite of his having refused until the last moment to adopt outright republicanism.

He became Minister of Finance and Justice in the provisional government which was set up immediately after the Revolution. As vice-chief of the provisional government he was second only to General Deodoro da Fon-

[3] Barbosa [Ruy]. *Prólogo y selección de Renato de Mendonça.* (El pensamiento de América, v 14) México, Secretaría de Educación Pública. 1944. p3-70.

seca, and since Deodoro was inclined to leave politics to the politicians, Barbosa was for a time the most influential leader in the government, in which were to be found such outstanding men as Benjamin Constant, Campos Salles and Quintino Bocayuva. It was he who wrote the decrees establishing religious liberty and separating Church and State. He also wrote the decree of 1890 establishing a federal republic. With Salvador Mendonça and Quintino Bocayuva he drafted the Constitution of 1891, which, incidentally, bore many resemblances to that of the United States. Barbosa himself remarked that it "is derived from the American, whose origin resides in the immemorial beginnings of English liberty." In *Os actos inconstitucionaes* (Unconstitutional Acts) he later wrote:

> The framers of the American Constitution, with whose sentiments the authors of the Brazilian Constitution were entirely at one, did all possible to establish in that instrument of limitation of powers an adequate check, not against the executive alone, but, and perhaps more pointedly, against the assemblies. More than a century ago, in relation to democracies, Madison showed that it is against the reckless ambitions of representative bodies that the nation must beware, must spare no precautions, and must exercise incessant vigilance. . . . Jefferson himself, the most thoroughly acquainted with all aspects of the French Revolution, inveighed against that menace.[4]

Criticism of some of Barbosa's financial measures, including the suppression of agricultural loans and his decree requiring payment of customs duties in gold, contributed to the overthrow of the ministry in 1891, and to Deodoro's withdrawal in favor of the vice president elected under the new constitution, Floriano Peixoto.

Although he continued on terms of close personal friendship with Peixoto, Barbosa soon became the frankest critic of the administration, leader of the opposition to what was properly considered a series of dictatorial acts of the new government. He undertook habeas corpus suits for forty-eight Brazilians arbitrarily arrested and exiled by the Peixoto government on political grounds. The Supreme Court denied the requests, with one judge dissenting. But while the suits were a failure, Barbosa had succeeded in making an issue of the government's disregard of constitutional rights. His work on the cases attracted international attention and his arguments were later published in the United States under the title *Martial Law*.

How far he had been successful in mobilizing public opinion appeared when he undertook habeas corpus proceedings in connection with another group of arbitrary arrests. This time he secured release for all except Admiral Wandenkolk and, carrying his plea for the Admiral to the senate, got from that body an endorsement of his views. In May 1893 he undertook the direction of the newspaper, *Jornal do Brasil,* and began in its pages an even broader campaign against the dictatorial measures of the government.

[4] Quoted by Charles William Turner, *op. cit.* p 110-11.

Although it appears that he was not actively involved, his newspaper campaign helped to inspire the naval revolt of September 6, 1893, and he was forced to flee, with his family, first to Buenos Aires, and from there to England. From England he continued his defense of constitutional liberties in a series of letters to the *Jornal do commercio*. After his return to Brazil in 1895 these letters were published in a volume, *Cartas de Inglaterra*. In these letters he extended his defense of civil liberties in Brazil with many references to British concepts and practices of law and liberty. While in England he also became interested in the case of Captain Dreyfus, whose trial appeared to him, as to so many other liberals, an obvious case of the miscarriage of justice in the interest of protecting certain anti-democratic and anti-Semitic interests in the French army. Barbosa was one of the first to take up the defense of Dreyfus, and his letter of January 7, 1895 appeared some time before Émile Zola's more famous *J'accuse*.

President Peixoto was succeeded by the constitutional regime of a civilian president, Prudente Moraes Barros of São Paulo, and Barbosa returned to Brazil in 1895. Although the immediate danger of dictatorship was past, he continued, from his seat in the senate, and in the press, to wage an unremitting campaign for constitutional government and liberty. His Bahian origin stood in the way of his reaching the presidency, since for political reasons, the presidents came generally from the two large states of São Paulo and Minas Geraes, particularly the former, during the early years of the republic. His opportunity came, however, in the election of 1910. General Hermes da Fonseca, nephew of the former president Deodoro da Fonseca, had been minister of war in the Penna government, and was the officially designated candidate. A military candidate raised the old specter of the revival of military dictatorship again, and the opposition forces united behind Barbosa to oppose Hermes da Fonseca. This was the background of what the Brazilians call the great *civilista* campaign of 1910. It was the greatest popular electoral campaign which Brazil had seen, and Barbosa's eloquence carried the plea against militarism in government the length and breadth of the land. He was clearly the popular candidate, but was defeated by the official control of the election machinery. He had many friends in army and navy circles, and some of them wished to lead a revolt. But Barbosa refused to let himself be swept off his feet by their offers. From his seat in the senate he denounced the official control of elections, but announced that he accepted the results, nevertheless. The army and navy will not revolt, he said. They had an "inviolable subordination to legally constituted authority. This is the true expression of *civilismo*. . . ."

This was a lesson in responsible statesmanship. Four years later he gave another. Brazil was suffering from a severe economic depression in 1913. A sharp reduction in the foreign markets for sugar, coffee, and rubber brought great hardship throughout the country. Barbosa was in the midst of an increasingly popular campaign for the presidency, when, near the end of the year, he renounced his candidacy in the interest of national harmony in a time of crisis, and backed the election of Wenceslau Brau. Ruy Barbosa was never elected president of his country, but he had set an example which was, perhaps, in the long run, a greater contribution than he could have made as chief executive.

Among the many achievements of this versatile man was a mastery of international law. This was shown in his selection by the Baron of Rio Branco, then foreign minister, to represent Brazil in the Second Hague Conference. It was the first appearance of a Latin American state at a world gathering, and the extent to which Barbosa and his colleagues influenced the deliberations and decisions of the Conference was, on this account, a particularly great tribute to his abilities. The European representatives knew him for his defense of the Dreyfus Case—which had now come to represent the line of division between liberals and conservatives in French politics, and, to a degree, in the politics of other countries as well. They were scarcely prepared for his great mastery of international law, and the indefatigable industry which caused him to take some part in the work of almost every commission of the Conference. It was a dramatic introduction of Brazil into the realm of world affairs.

His interest turned increasingly to international affairs. After 1897 he became one of the leading advocates of an international organization, or league of nations. When war came in 1914 he favored the Allied cause, and urged the development of a new concept of neutrality based upon the obligations undertaken at The Hague. In 1916, speaking to the students and faculties of the University of Buenos Aires on the occasion of the centenary of Argentine independence, he said: "The term neutrality has a new mission. . . . It is now the moral vindication of written law. It will, therefore, be an organized neutrality . . . to impose just rights." He was stating the concept of neutrality in World War II. In one other respect, also, he foreshadowed the shape of things to come. When the question of an armistice was in the air in October 1918, he wrote in *O imparcial,* cautioning against permitting Germany to make peace in such a way that she might later claim she was not really defeated. President Rodrigues Alves asked him to head the Brazilian delegation to the Peace Conference at Paris. But he was spared what might well have been a deeply disillusioning experience in comparison with the conference of 1907. He asked to be excused for personal and political reasons.

On March 1, 1923 death claimed one of Brazil's greatest personalities and statesmen. Probably no other Brazilian better represented the ideals and aspirations of the republican revolution. Certainly none other gave more eloquent expression to its republican ideals or to the constitutional rights of citizens of the republic. He was Brazil's foremost spokesman of democracy.

Barbosa [Ruy]. Prólogo y selección de Renato de Mendonça. (El pensamiento de América, v 14) México, Secretaría de Educación. 1944. 251p.

Crawford, W. Rex. A century of Latin-American thought. Cambridge, Harvard University Press. 1944. p 190-3.

Henríquez Ureña, Pedro. Literary currents in Hispanic America. Cambridge, Harvard University Press. 1945. p 137-60.

Justiça (Porto Alegre, Brazil). May-June, September-October, and November-December. 1943. (p279-323, 509-35, 621-42). Rui Barbosa. João Mangabeira.

Lima Barbosa, Mario de. Ruy Barbosa no politica e na historia, 1849-1914. Rio de Janeiro, F. Briguiet. 1916. 420p.

Pires, Homero. As influencias politicas anglo-americanas em Rui Barbosa. [Rio de Janeiro] Instituto Brasil-Estados Unidos. [1942] 22p.

Turner, Charles William. Ruy Barbosa, Brazilian crusader for the essential freedoms. Nashville, Tenn. Abingdon-Cokesbury. 1945. 208p.

PART II

LEADERS OF THOUGHT

JOSÉ JOAQUÍN FERNÁNDEZ DE LIZARDI (1776-1827)

"El Pensador Mexicano"

One of the most vigorous and effective pens wielded in the cause of democracy and liberal reform during the years of the Mexican movement for independence was that of Fernández de Lizardi, better known by his self-adopted sobriquet, and the name of his journal, *The Mexican Thinker* (*El pensador mexicano*). For seventeen years (1810-1827) the most critical formative years of the Mexican nation, he voiced the aspirations of those Mexicans who rebelled against Spanish traditionalism, authoritarianism, fanaticism, and ecclesiasticism and hoped, by sweeping clean with the broom of reform to erect a new, free, and American society in Mexico. His tall, slender, stooped figure, and dark, pale and friendly face, pierced by startling black eyes, became the symbol of this cause. In literature, also, he spoke with the new voice of American independence from authority, and his picaresque novel, *El periquillo sarniento* [1] has been called the first truly Mexican book.

His participation in the Mexican movement for independence has a double significance. He represents the new power of the press in Spanish America, as well as the spirit of unrest and newly conscious Americanism of the creoles, their strong sense of the evils and injustice of the Spanish colonial system, their great ambition to dominate a political scene of their own making while fearing the effects of political freedom upon the ignorant masses, and their optimistic haste to remake the social order overnight by democratic agitation, ecclesiastical reform, and general education. It is the tendency today—a tendency into which it is all too easy to fall—to dismiss agitators like Fernández de Lizardi as quixotic, unduly optimistic, and impractical. But in some respects this is not a fair judgment. In this very uncompromising optimism lies the source of much that we recognize as most essential to the American spirit. If their efforts were less successful in organizing a democratic and prosperous society in the Latin American than in the Anglo-American scene it was due only in part to the fact that the Latin American ideology was more radical and less practical than that of northern America. In part their lack of success must be attributed to the greater difficulty of the ethnic, economic, and political problems of Latin America and to the greater strength of the forces of traditionalism and colonialism there. The career of Fernández de Lizardi shows at many points that a partial realization of the magnitude of these problems, con-

---

[1] A partial English translation, by Katherine Anne Porter, was published under the title *The Itching Parrot*. New York, Doubleday, Doran and Co. 1942. 290p.

tradictory as it may seem, was frequently an obstacle to the adoption of clear-cut political positions and to vigorous consistent political action.

Fernández de Lizardi was an apostle of the new French and North American ideas, a partisan of independence although long calling himself a royalist, an advocate of popular education to eliminate ignorance and religious fanaticism, an opponent of Negro slavery and of the privileges of the nobility. Once freed from the royalism of the early years of his public career, he urged a federal democratic republic for Mexico and fought for religious tolerance, the correction of clerical abuses, and freedom of the press. In the skill and untiring energy with which he wielded the newly discovered power of the press he resembles Marat although in other respects his career differs greatly from that of the French revolutionary journalist. In the last years of his life he pitted this power of the press against the Church, the most powerful institution of Mexican society, with all the confidence of a Marat, and when attacked by the clergy for his defense of Freemasonry, he replied: "If there are pulpits in which they attack me, presses do not lack for my defense."

His early life and education were typical of the youth of the small creole middle class which was appearing in Mexican society by the end of the eighteenth century. His father was a physician who, probably because he was unable to earn a sufficient living in Mexico City, found it necessary, shortly after the birth of José in 1776, to move to the small provincial town of Tepotzotlán. As a young boy José attended a school in his home town. Later he was sent to Mexico City to study Latin with Don Manuel Enríquez de Agreda, and, subsequently, to follow the course in philosophy with Dr. Manuel San Cristoval y Garay. Shortly before the time of examination for his baccalaureate degree, his father was taken ill and he had to return to Tepotzotlán to assist him. This was some time before 1798. Meanwhile, his early tendency to revolt against parental and other authority, as well as something of the character of his father, perhaps, is shown in the fact that he was cited to the Inquisition by his father for amusing himself with an "amatory card game."

Little is known of his life between the years 1798 and the appearance of his earliest known published poem, *La polaca*, in 1809. For some reason Fernández de Lizardi chose to be very secretive concerning these years. Paul Radin, who has made the most careful study of the question, concludes that they were busy years in which he assisted his father, acted as an amanuensis, served as a minor political official in Taxco and Acapulco, and devoted himself to study and to writing. Many of his poems, published later, must have been written during these years.[2]

[2] See Paul Radin, ed. *An Annotated Bibliography of the Poems and Pamphlets of J. J. Fernandez de Lizardi*. San Francisco, California State Library. 1940. 2v. (mimeographed) p 1-7, 14.

About 1805 or 1806 he married Dolores Orenday. They had one child, a daughter, but later took with their family two orphan boys. Sometime in the early years of the new century he returned to Mexico City. González Obregón is inclined to accept the notion that he was a frequent visitor in the home of Doña Josefa Ortiz de Domínguez during the time when her home was the center of the discussions of independence which helped bring on the rebellion led by the priest Miguel Hidalgo in 1810, but this is a pure guess, and is very unlikely.

It seems reasonably certain that he was in sympathy with the Hidalgo uprising in 1810, and that he was a friend of some of its leaders. If we are to accept his later statements as true, however, it was against his will and better judgment that he found himself in command of a small body of rebel forces which was captured by the loyalists toward the end of the year. The excesses and violence of the insurgents, particularly in the massacre at Guanajuato, apparently had caused him to turn against the movement. He was able to convince the authorities that he had refused a colonelcy offered him by the rebels and had, in fact, only acted under compulsion. He was freed, but ever after was suspected, with reason, of sympathy for the rebellion. This brief experience seems to have convinced him that he was not suited for the role of military leader. From the end of 1810 until he joined the forces of Iturbide in 1821 he took no direct part in the actual revolutionary movements, although he became increasingly important as a spokesman of the growing Mexican discontent.

By 1810 he had acquired his own press and soon began to publish his own writings, a practice for which he was severely attacked by his critics. Two poems, among others published in 1811, *La verdad pelada* and *La muralla de México*, immediately attracted wide attention and brought severe criticism for their unorthodox form, their appeal to popular taste, and their satire on social conditions of the times. By the end of the year some of his poems had appeared in the *Diario de México*, and had been both attacked and defended by critics. He was thus already a figure of literary prominence when he began the publication of *El pensador mexicano* in 1812.

The Spanish Constitution of 1812 established freedom of press and provided the opportunity for the social and occasionally political criticisms with which Fernández de Lizardi filled the journal, or as it might more accurately be styled, the series of pamphlets which made "El Pensador" a personage known to all the Mexican reading public. It was his principal forum for increasingly severe attacks on the Spanish colonial regime. He announced his intention to prove the Spanish government to be the worst possible government. Yet, strange as it may seem, until the days of Iturbide he remained a monarchist, perhaps for expediency's sake, and he never seemed to be fundamentally anti-Spanish, however much he criticized the abuses of Spanish authority.

"There is no civilized nation which has had worse government than ours (worse in America)," he wrote, "nor vassals who have suffered more vigorously the chains of tyranny." Yet he could not excuse the followers of Hidalgo for their excesses and their wanton destruction. "The virtue of the revolution has departed," he wrote in a poem of 1811, *A Patriotic Warning to the Insurgents.* Yet, he said, it was not only Hidalgo but the Spanish enemies of any renovation who had "burned our towns, sacrificed our sons and produced the turmoil in this continent."

His writings up to this point show that Fernández de Lizardi had absorbed many of the rationalist and equalitarian ideas of the new revolutionary thought. Some of these influences no doubt can be traced back to his days in the Colegio de San Ildefonso, where he associated, for example, with Antonio Pérez Alamillo and Juan Antonio Montenegro, two priests who were later brought before the Inquisition and admonished for their radical democratic ideas. He believed in a classless society in which there would be complete freedom for the individual to advance according to his merit. He was cautious, as noted, in advancing his democratic ideas during these early years, because of his distrust of the violence of the current revolutionary movements. Yet the colloquial and popular style of his writings gave even to his criticism of the foibles of Mexican society a revolutionary flavor which the frightened conservative rulers of Mexico were quick to detect.

By December 1812 *El pensador mexicano* was the most talked-of journal in Mexico. Fernández de Lizardi's rise to fame had been meteoric, and his popular influence was felt wherever Mexicans read. The seventh issue of *El pensador*, dedicated to the viceroy, and asking for the revocation of a decree ordering the military trial of revolutionary priests, was too much for the government, and it brought about his arrest. Although he had carefully avoided any direct or open connection with the revolutionists under Morelos he was clearly suspected of such connections, and the official court records tend to reinforce the view that he had at least some contact with them.

His arrest on December 9, 1812, and the seven months in prison which followed, ruined him financially and dampened his spirit as an agitator for several years. He continued to publish *El pensador* through 1814, but was largely content to limit himself to literary matters, criticism of customs and manners, and to writing of the necessity of free general education.

In 1814 he presented a comprehensive national plan for free and obligatory education. Mexico's educational backwardness, he wrote, was the fault of the town clergy and town authorities. The schools suffered from poorly trained teachers, and a program of teacher training was a first necessity for improving the school system. He urged reform of school discipline and adequate physical training for all children before entering school. In the spirit of Rousseau's *Émile* and of Pestalozzi, he proposed teaching by objects. If necessary, he urged, the authorities should give clothing to pupils so that parents could not keep children from school on the pretext that they could not afford to clothe them properly.

Such an educational program was too much to hope for in light of the conditions of the weak colonial regime of Mexico in 1814. In fact Mexico was to wait more than a century before realizing a program such as Fernández de Lizardi proposed. Yet utopian as it seemed, universal education was not at all an impractical proposal for Mexico in 1814, if only the political and economic problems of Mexican life could have been settled by the establishment of a stable political regime. Fernández de Lizardi's proposal is clear evidence that reformers of his day saw the essential role which education must play in the construction of a democratic society. But the intransigence of their attacks on clericalism and traditionalism, by widening the breach between the reformers and the conservative elements of Mexican society essential to achieving political stability, helped, in some respects, to bring on the years of chaos and anarchy which followed in Mexico.

The restoration of Ferdinand VII to the Spanish throne brought suppression of freedom of the press and discontinuance of El pensador. Although Fernández de Lizardi continued to bring out many of his writings as serials or periodicals, he was forced to turn even more to literary rather than social and political subjects. In 1815 he published the Alacena de frioleras, a miscellany of fables and articles on Mexican customs. In 1816 he began publishing in sections his most successful novel, El periquillo sarniento (The Itching Parrot). This picaresque novel, considered by many Mexican critics to mark the beginning of a new and American tendency in Mexican letters, was a facile instrument in the hands of El pensador for subtle but increasingly sharp attacks upon the colonial regime. Permission to print the fourth volume of the novel was forbidden because it urged abolition of slavery.

The Revolution of 1820 in Spain and a new constitution restored freedom of the press. Fernández de Lizardi at once started a journal, El conductor eléctrico, to defend the new Spanish constitution. It was a complicated situation in which he found himself. He had consistently believed that it was necessary for Mexico to free herself from the social and political dominance of Spain, but during the years 1813 to 1820 he had usually felt that this could be done within the Spanish tradition as it had developed in Mexico, and under the Spanish monarchy. The new constitution seemed at first to offer a prospect of this kind of evolutionary development. But it soon became evident that strong reactionary influences in Mexico, under the leadership of Canon Matías Monteagudo, planned to suppress the constitution by seizing power. The military leader selected for their purpose was the recently retired Augustín Iturbide. The story of how Iturbide, when sent against the rebel leader Guerrero, came to terms with him instead, and proclaimed the independence of Mexico, is too well known to warrant being repeated here. Whether or not Iturbide betrayed his reactionary backers is still a subject of historical controversy.

But these developments had created a dangerous and complicated situation in 1821 in which the most diverse political groups favored independence for quite opposite reasons. Fernández de Lizardi always claimed that he had proclaimed independence in March 1821, in his pamphlet *Chamorro y Dominiquín*, a week before Iturbide's proclamation of the Plan of Iguala. He had been imprisoned for this publication, and naturally became a warm supporter of the new movement and its leaders, as did most of the Mexican liberals at first. Later he was disillusioned with Iturbide's rule, and attacked him vehemently. Yet he never could forget that Iturbide had been the instrument of Mexican independence, and often in his later writings defended him as the victim of the reactionary elements which surrounded him.

His career as an agitator for reform was by no means ended with the achievement of Mexican independence. During the next few years, and almost until his death in 1827, he was the center of the most bitter controversy of his life. As already noticed, he criticized Iturbide severely after the latter revealed reactionary tendencies. In a series of pamphlets he urged freedom of the press and proposed the organization of a federal republic, while continuing his attack on clericalism and the privileges and wealth of the Church.

Among the many questions which quickly arose to divide the widely divergent factions united temporarily under the Plan of Iguala, one of the bitterest was the issue of Freemasonry. In 1822 the bulls of Clement XII and Benedict XIV of the preceding century, condemning Freemasonry, were published in Mexico. Fernández de Lizardi immediately took up the issue in a pamphlet, *Defense of the Freemasons*. The result was his excommunication and a series of vicious, and perhaps officially inspired press attacks against him. He appealed to the congress to set aside the excommunication and continued to argue the cause of freemasonry in a series of pamphlets, *Letters to the Papist*, and *Second Defense of the Freemasons*. Not until after the proclamation of the republic, however, did he seek and secure grudging absolution from the Church.

Meanwhile, in a pamphlet whimsically entitled *Un fraile sale a bailar y la música no es mala* (A friar begins to dance and the music is not bad), he presented his strongest argument for religious tolerance. He called on the republican congress to adopt religious tolerance and to regulate the clergy lest they "involve us in a new war."

During the years 1824 and 1825 he published a series of *Conversations of del Payo with the Sacristan,* in which he set forth clearly the radical ideas of the small but determined party of reformers which was struggling for control of the new Mexican republic. He proposed a liberal constitution on the federal principle, in which the Church was to be used as an instrument of education for democracy. According to Article 87 of his constitution the clergy would be required, in their Sunday sermons, to teach that all men are by nature free, that civil authority is necessary to defend the weak against the strong, and that from this subjection to civil authority arises true liberty, which is freedom to do good and fear of doing evil; that according to the Scriptures all men are brothers and fellow citizens, and so should not quarrel over differences of religious opinions, since intolerance proves only the pride and lack of knowledge of their own religion of those who defend it; that everyone should obey good laws and cultivate wholesome customs, since virtue brings its reward, and vice its punishment even in this life. Thus, he urged, men will fulfill the duty imposed by God, Nature, and Society.

The next three years were among the busiest of his life. For a time he edited another journal, *La gaceta.* About this time, too, he published the first two volumes of *La quijotita y su prima,* a novel dealing with the education of women. *La quijotita* was not published in complete form until after his death. He also wrote another novel in the picaresque style of *El periquillo sarniento, The Life and Adventures of Don Catrín de la Rachenda,* which was published posthumously. Pamphlets continued to come from his pen in large numbers, if not in the flood of the years 1821-1823, until his death in 1827 from pulmonary tuberculosis, from which he had suffered for a long time.

Fernández de Lizardi is one of the founders of Mexican national literature. He was also a pioneer in establishing public libraries. In 1820 he organized a Public Reading Society, where for one *real,* periodicals and books could be read or borrowed. But he is equally important as one of the principal intellectual leaders of democratic reform in the early days of Mexican independence. There is no suggestion of personal political ambition in his career. Nor, apparently, was he a person to inspire confidence as a practical political leader. Friend and intimate of most of the prominent leaders of Mexican independence, he was content to wield the power of ideas and the printed word, with which he made a lasting impression on the Mexico of his day. Fortunately he did not live to experience the disillusionment of the reformers after their failure in 1833, a disillusionment of which his fears of the illiterate Mexican masses provided many premonitions.

González Obregón, Luis. Don José Joaquín Fernández de Lizardi (El pensador mexicano). México, Secretaría de Fomento. 1888. 91p. Rev. ed. México, Botas. 1938. 223p.
Norall, Frank Victor. The ideology of Fernández de Lizardi as revealed in El periquillo sarniento (MS thesis). University of Chicago. 1941.

Radin, Paul, ed.   An annotated bibliography of the poems and pamphlets
of J. J. Fernández de Lizardi.   Prepared by the personnel of the WPA
project no. 665-08-3-236.   San Francisco, California State Library.
1940.   In two parts.   179p.   (mimeographed)   (The third part appeared
in The Hispanic American Historical Review. 29:284-291. May 1946.
Radin, Paul, ed.   The opponents and friends of Lizardi.   San Francisco,
California State Library.   1939.   134p. (mimeographed)
Spell, Jefferson Rea.   The life and works of José Joaquín Fernández de
Lizardi.   Philadelphia, University of Pennsylvania Press. 1931. 141p.

ANDRÉS BELLO (1781-1865)

THE CIVILIZER

Germán Arciniegas, the Colombian historian and critic, has recently given a vivid portrayal of the thought and influence of this fellow citizen and friend of Bolívar.[1] Andrés Bello was one of three great leaders given to the independence movement by Venezuela, and, all things considered, he was its greatest intellectual. An excellent poet in his own right, he made lasting contributions to the understanding of the genius and forms of Spanish poetry, as well as to the development of an American literature and an American literary criticism in Chile, his adopted country. His writings on Spanish grammar freed the study of that subject from the domination of Latin grammar, and won acceptance by the Spanish Academy. The Chilean national code of laws was the product of his mind and pen more than that of any other individual,while his writings upon that subject and on international law were profound formative influences upon the Latin American mind. The National University of Chile is a lasting, and probably the greatest, monument to his memory.

He was born in Caracas on November 29, 1781, as scholars have discovered since his death. Strangely enough, he himself seems never to have known the exact date of his birth. His family was of modest means and known particularly for its devotion to art and music. His mother, Antonia Amunátegui, came from a distinguished family. His father, Bartolomé Bello, was a lawyer and a musical composer of note. One of his father's masses was still sung in the churches of Caracas at the end of the nineteenth century.

It is indicative of the high state of cultural development in Venezuela at the end of the eighteenth century that one of the greatest Spanish humanists since the days of the Renaissance, and the greatest of Latin America, should have received all of his formal education in Venezulan schools. His first teacher, Cristóbal de Quesada, a Mercedarian friar, taught him grammar and instilled in him a great love for literature, so that all his life he lived in close association with great books. It was characteristic that he should remember, as one of his most important youthful experiences, the discovery of Cervantes' Don Quijote. In the Colegio de Santa Rosa he came under the teaching of Dr. José Antonio Montenegro, who seems to have had the effect of awakening more than one bright young mind in the Caracas of his day. He learned French from a grammar given him as a gift, and began,

[1] El pensamiento vivo de Andrés Bello. Buenos Aires, Losada. 1946. 214p.

at this early age, to establish direct contact with French thought of the eighteenth century. He also learned English and read Shakespeare and Locke's *On Human Understanding*.

At the age of sixteen he entered the university, studying law and, to some extent, medicine. The presbyter Rafael Escalona, one of the noted teachers of the time, was his instructor in philosophy. To help pay his expenses he tutored children of families of wealth, among them the future Liberator, Simón Bolívar, whom he taught geography. The association with Bolívar, thus begun, remained a close one until the latter's untimely death. It contributed not a little to Bello's prestige, and was one of his most cherished recollections in after years. Another great formative influence in his life was the visit of Baron Alexander von Humboldt and his companion, the French naturalist Aimé Bonpland, to Caracas toward the end of 1799. To the young man of Caracas the frequent long walks with these two world travelers and men of science not only opened up a whole new world of experience and observation, but brought new insight as well into the general state of affairs in Spanish America and its unrealized potentialities.

In 1802 he was given a post in the office of the governor, Manuel de Guevara Vasconcelos, and in 1807 received an honorary position, by royal appointment, as commissioner of war. Vasconcelos, who had made himself in a sense the protector of the brilliant young student, soon died. But his successor, Juan de Casas, kept Bello in his position. When a copy of the London *Times* brought the first news of the abdication of Charles IV and his son from the Spanish crown, it was Bello's translation which first made the events known in the captaincy. A few days later Napoleon's envoys arrived and he served as translator at their meeting with Governor Casas. Shortly thereafter he conveyed to them the governor's advice to leave the country.

He was a frequent visitor in the Ustáriz family circle, famous for its literary interests, and in that of the Bolívar family, in both of which the new and radical ideas of the day were discussed. As a result, when the premature conspiracy of 1810, which involved Bolívar, was denounced, Bello was suspected of having given away the secret. It was an unjust accusation, however, and one which he always denied. No evidence has ever been brought out to prove that he had any part in exposing the plot, and his continued friendly relations with Bolívar, as well as his participation in the government of the junta established on April 19, 1810 argue against it.

The junta sent him on a mission to London in June of the same year, as secretary of a commission composed of Simón Bolívar and Luis López Méndez. It was a mission which achieved little diplomatic success, since Britain was at this time allied with Spain, and unwilling to take any positive steps favoring the independence of the Spanish colonies. Its one success was in persuading Francisco Miranda to set out for Venezuela. Bolívar soon returned to America, but Bello stayed on in London, representing the interests of Venezuela and later those of the union of Venezuela and New Granada in the Bolivarian Great Colombia, as well as those of Chile after its independence. He remained for nineteen years, years of uncertainty, of alternating hope and despair, as the fortunes of independence waxed and waned. After the success of Bolívar in northern South America, the financial and political difficulties of the new governments which Bello now represented gave rise to other kinds of trouble. His pay was usually in arrears, while his letters to the Liberator, who was now preoccupied with the internal problems of the unstable political structure over which he presided precariously, brought little or no response. Feeling that his native country and his friends had forgotten him, his feelings hurt at the offer of what he considered an inferior post, that of Colombian consul-general in Paris, Bello accepted an invitation of the government of Chile to come to that country as an under-secretary for foreign affairs. Bolívar's conscience-stricken note begging him to remain in the service of Gran Colombia, "the least evil which America has," arrived after he had set sail for Chile.

His mind had matured under the stimulating influence of nineteenth century English thought and of personal contacts with some of its greatest minds. Miranda had introduced him widely in British society. He came to know, among others, Jeremy Bentham and James Mill. He haunted the British Museum and learned to draw on its rich resources for studies over a wide range of subjects. His later works on grammar, on the codification of laws, and on the literary origins of *The Cid*, would have been impossible in Chile except for the researches which he carried on at this time. With several fellow Spanish Americans, notably the Ecuadorian poet, José Joaquín Olmedo, he founded two reviews in London for the purpose of making Spanish America and its people better known. The pages of *La biblioteca americana* and *El repertorio americano* covered a wide range of subjects, indicating the broad interests of the editors. There were original poems and articles of literary criticism and philology, as well as scientific articles and projects for social and political reforms.

Bello was forty-seven years of age when he left England. His children had been born there and his first wife, Mary Ana Boyland, had died there a few years after their marriage in 1814. Now he was accompanied by a second English wife, Isabel Dunn, who was to be a constant tie with England and things English during the years to come. He was a man mature in years and bearing. Confident of himself, he spoke in a pleasant but grave voice, with a dignified mien, and with the elegant gestures and the manners of a man accustomed to the ways of the ruling classes of his day, both in Venezuela and in England. A broad forehead surmounted oval eyes, eyes which looked out with calm assurance. His hair was scant and light, while an eagle-like nose, fine lips, and a round beard completed an appearance which one could not fail to remark.

Few scholars have enjoyed the unique opportunity which Bello was to have in Chile—the opportunity to shape the development of a new nation almost from the beginning. Still rarer, however, is the singular combination of intellectual and personal characteristics, with the prestige of having conducted affairs of diplomacy during the trying years of the revolutionary wars, which enabled him, a foreigner, to become the center of a great program of national reform and cultural development. Even the fact that he had been invited to Chile by the liberal government of President Pinto seemed scarcely to stand in the way of his immediately achieving a position of importance under the conservative regime established by President Prieto and the minister-dictator, Diego Portales.[2] This is particularly difficult to understand until it is noted that many former liberals, including Mariano Egaña, who was primarily responsible for bringing Bello to Chile, joined with the conservatives in forming the new administration.

Bello has been called opportunistic, even reactionary, because of his willingness to cooperate with the conservatives after they had overthrown the liberals and suppressed the constitution of 1828. But such a judgment fails to understand Bello's concept of his role in the national life. As a foreigner he wisely remained aloof from party politics. Yet, despite his political neutrality, perhaps even because of it, he linked the conservative regime with the cause of reform in many ways. Indeed, no small share of the statesmanlike success achieved by the conservative alliance of commercial and landed interests which dominated Chile almost unchallenged for the succeeding three decades was due to the quiet, unobtrusive, but all-pervading influence of this adopted son of Chile. In the main, he influenced foreign policy, juridical development, national education, and the development of Chilean culture, rather than the course of political events. Yet in various indirect ways his influence impinged upon practically every important aspect of national life at one time or another.

During most of the time, from his arrival in Chile in 1829 until 1852, he was the chief counselor of the government on matters of foreign policy, first as *oficial mayor*, and later as sub-secretary in charge of foreign affairs. Diego Portales relied greatly upon his advice, and two subsequent chancellors, Manuel Montt and José Joaquín Pérez (both of whom later reached the presidency) found him their principle mainstay in that office. He drafted notes and treaties, guiding the formulation of Chilean policy along lines of international law, a subject which he had begun to study while an official in the captaincy-general of Venezuela. In Chile he had begun al-

---

[2] In 1829 the Pinto administration gave way to the shortlived liberal and personal administration of Francisco Ramón Vicuña. The fall of the liberals was the result both of their own disunity and of the political intrigues of Portales and Prieto.

most at once to teach this subject in the University of San Felipe. His textbook, which first appeared in 1832, was soon translated into French and German, and remains one of the great American contributions in this field.[3] Some of the principles of neutrality which he was responsible for including in a treaty with Peru in 1835 were subsequently adopted at the Conference of Paris in 1856.

Portales ruled with the most severe dictatorship in the history of Chile, suppressing liberal revolts harshly, while controlling his own followers with a thinly gloved hand of iron. Much of this must have been distasteful in a high degree to Bello, whose concepts of liberty were formed, in part at least, in the British mold. Still he saw, as did many other former liberals, like Mariano Egaña, who now supported the conservative government, that Portales ruled with an eye to building political structure for the future: that he knew how to use outstanding men of moderate and liberal views as well as those of more conservative character. It was Egaña who had drafted the constitution of 1833, and Bello had assisted him in the task. He is generally credited with the authorship of those clauses of the constitution incorporating the principles of the French Revolution relating to guaranties of individual rights.

This aspect of the Portales regime helps to explain Bello's adjustment to it. He was not serving the cause of reaction, but the cause of moderate reform within a conservative government. To be sure, as a humanist, he was conservative in the sense of having the greatest respect for a rich cultural tradition. Stability and order, to his mind, were first essentials for the great work of cultural development which he envisaged in the Chilean nation. But they were only a means to an end—steppingstones to a progressive program of reforms, and not an end in themselves. Moreover, there is abundant evidence in his whole career, as well as throughout his writing— in practically every topic upon which he touched—that he considered it necessary for Chile to make a clear break with much of her colonial heritage and tradition in order to build the American and national institutions and culture essential to her progress. Bello might, therefore, best be styled a moderate liberal.

Among the many achievements of a long and fruitful lifetime—he lived to be nearly eighty-four—it is difficult to single out the greatest. But certainly one which stands out among his greatest achievements is the codification of Chilean law. It also illustrates well the caution and the long-range planning with which he approached an important objective. As early as 1833 he had written in *La araucana* (the government-supported organ with which he was associated from the time of its beginning) of the great need for codification if the guaranties of the constitution were to be carried

[3] The definitive edition of this work, *Principios de derecho internacional,* was published in Santiago in 1864. It may be found in *Obras completas.* Official edition, 1881-93. v 10.

out. Various proposals for codification were made during the years which followed, but political complications and conservative forces in the government prevented their being followed up. Meanwhile, Bello, on his own account, began to work privately on the project. He had two volumes ready, one on the law of inheritance and one on contracts, when, from his seat in the senate in 1840,[4] he proposed a legislative commission on codification. His proposal was adopted and he became the senatorial member of the commission.

Criticisms and objections were many and strong. Bello met them patiently with arguments in *La araucana*, and in patient discussions with a second commission set up to pass upon the work of the first. He described the task of codification as no more difficult for the Chileans, and just as important for their national development, as was the drawing up of the *Siete Partidas* for thirteenth-century Spain. His two preliminary volumes were the basis upon which the commission began its work, and much of the subsequent painstaking labor likewise fell upon him. Strangely enough, he had never been licensed as a lawyer, although in England he had studied comparative law and had written on legal matters. Moreover, in 1836, he had received one of the last titles of bachelor of sacred canons and laws awarded by the University of San Felipe.

The work of codification was completed by 1852, although the code was not given full effect until three years later. Bello had given over twenty years of the most careful, patient work to this task. With typical thoroughness he had consulted all the important magistrates and tribunals of the nation in the course of those years. In its final form the code consisted of four books devoted to (1) persons, (2) property, (3) inheritance and gifts, and (4) general obligations and contracts. These four volumes were divided into 94 titles and 2525 articles. The code shows considerable originality, but its outstanding trait is its essentially practical character resulting from the masterly way in which the rich resources of the Spanish and civil law were drawn upon to form a code suited to the needs of the new nation. In this practical character and in its sound legal basis it resembles the somewhat earlier criminal code of Vasconcellos in Brazil. Both had wide influence throughout America.

The Colegio de Santiago had been founded by the conservatives in 1829 to oppose the liberal Liceo de Santiago of José Joaquín de Mora, best known for his editorship of the *Mercurio chileno*, and for his authorship of the liberal constitution of 1828. Like Bello, the Spaniard Mora had been brought to Chile by the liberal government of President Pinto, largely through the influence of Mariano Egaña. With the fall of the liberals, the rector of the Colegio, Juan Francisco Meneses, entered the ministry of the conservatives and Bello was named to take his place. He immediately be-

---

[4] He had been appointed to the senate in 1837.

came involved in a controversy with Mora and his followers. Beginning as an argument over Spanish grammar, it soon took on political tone, and helped drive Mora on to attacks upon Portales and the conservatives after official funds were withdrawn from the Liceo. These attacks soon brought about Mora's exile from Chile. The Colegio de Santiago did not long survive the Liceo, for official funds for its support were soon withdrawn also. The controversy in itself was not significant, but it shows how little confidence the conservatives had in Bello in these first years, at least in the field of education.

The establishment of the University of Chile was in no small degree his work. Mariano Egaña, as minister, had initiated the plan, but it was Manuel Montt who, as minister of instruction, called upon Bello to draft a plan for the establishment of a national university. After a long debate in congress, and considerable modification of the original plan, especially in the direction of more governmental control, the university was established in 1843. The selection of Bello as the first rector, in competition with the former head of the Royal University of San Felipe, was a great tribute to the personal prestige and reputation which he had acquired in his fourteen years of residence in Chile. He had, indeed, become the outstanding intellectual figure of Chile, and his inauguration, which took the form of a personal ovation, was the high point of his long and successful career.

His inaugural address outlined a national program of education, research, and cultural development. It called for a national program of primary education such as he had frequently urged in La araucana, but at the same time emphasized the importance of higher literary and scientific studies as its necessary basis. In the field of law, he pointed out, the government expected from the university "practical utility, positive results, [and] social improvements." The program of the university in economics should be "completely Chilean," examining the results of Chilean statistics, and studying Chilean society from the economic standpoint. In similar vein he spoke in reference to medicine, the sciences, language (emphasizing the study of the Spanish language), arts, and literature. Especially noteworthy was his plea for the writing of Chilean poetry. It was a great plea for freedom from subservience to European ideas and educational models—for the development of a national culture which was American.

His friends were well represented in the University. Manuel Egaña was the first dean of the faculty of law. José Victorino Lastarria, his former student, whose fighting journal, El crepúsculo (The Twilight) devoted to literary, political and social liberty, was founded the same year, was his principal lieutenant in the University and soon became dean of the faculty of humanities. Salvador Sanfuentes, a great poet, and another former student, was the University's first secretary. As head of the newly established normal school, Domingo F. Sarmiento, the future schoolteacher-president of Argentina, and author of *Facundo,* came under the broad direction of the University. Two of the greatest minds of Latin America in the nineteenth century were thus brought together, but not always in agreement. Bello's debate with Sarmiento over language in 1842 was one of the great literary arguments of the age in America. In fact the two men saw eye to eye on very few questions. Bello was also responsible for bringing into the University the great Polish physicist, Ignacio Domeyko, who eventually became rector after Bello's death in 1865.

For twenty-two years, frequently under great difficulty, Bello carried on a long and ultimately successful campaign for the independence of the University, to free it from the political restraints which originated at the beginning of the University's existence with the suppression of the teaching of *derecho público* (public law). With his natural instinct to support law and order, he was not one to indulge in frequent vain protests. Yet time and again he threw the support of his own prestige and that of the University behind the liberal ideas of his younger colleagues, and eventually great gains were made in its freedom from political restraint.

As a scholar Bello is best known for his grammar of the Spanish language, published in 1857. The revolutionary effect of this book and its recognition by the Spanish Academy have already been remarked. In addition to ending, once and for all, the artificial domination of Latin grammatical forms and rules over the Spanish language, he succeeded in bringing about general acceptance of the principle that language changed and developed in accordance with certain recognizable principles related to the genius of the language. He defended the right of the Americas to participate in the evolution of the mother tongue, yet one of his major objectives was to prevent this resulting in the development of separate dialects, with the resultant "corruption" of language. Much of his philology would not be accepted by contemporary scientific students of language, to be sure, yet he stated one surprisingly modern principle in applying, as a criterion of good usage, the use of any expression by contemporary writers of good taste and erudition.

His critical writings on Spanish poetry were almost equally important, and had a significant influence on the development of modern Spanish verse, and particularly that of Chile. As early as 1827, while in London, in an article which he wrote for *El repertorio americano,* he had traced the use of assonance in Spanish poetry to its widespread use in medieval French and Spanish verse, and thence to Latin. His defence of the use of assonance cleared the way for the development of one of the outstanding traits of modern Spanish verse. The Spanish critic Menéndez y Pelayo, and others, have called him the greatest poet of Chile. His early poem *La agricultura de la zona torrida* (1826) pointed the way for American poets to draw their images and ideas from the American soil. It was prophetic of the great influence he was to exercise in Chile, giving rise to a school of poets in a country which had none before, properly speaking. The great Chilean poets who followed, Salvador Sanfuentes, Guillermo Blest, Eduardo de la Barra, González Bastías, Gabriela Mistral, and Pablo Neruda show his influence in their works.

He encouraged the great literary movement of 1842 with his bold invitation to Lastarria to deliver before the University in 1844 the address which became known as the declaration of Spanish American literary independence. The codification of Chilean law and the University of Chile are monuments to his lasting achievements such as few men of modern times can equal. But perhaps his greatest achievement lay in the influence which he exercised over other men. Chileans who had experienced his teaching—José Victorino Lastarria, Salvador Sanfuentes, Benjamín Vicuña Mackenna, Manuel Antonio Matta, Isidoro Errájuriz and Domingo Santa María—were the leaders of Chilean liberal thought and politics in the next generation. Two of them became presidents of the nation. This is not only convincing evidence of the profound spirit of liberalism which moved in and through his acceptance of the existing conservative regime in Chile, it is also the basis for his well deserved title of the Civilizer of Chile.

Andrés Bello, ed. by Gabriel Méndez Plancarte. (Serie el pensamiento de América, 8) México, Secretaría de Educación Pública. 1943. 197p.

Amunátegui, Miguel Luis. Vida de Don Andrés Bello. Santiago de Chile, Ramírez. 1882. 672p.

Arciniegas, Germán. El pensamiento vivo de Andrés Bello. Buenos Aires, Losada. 1946. 214p.

Bello, Andrés. Obras completas. Santiago de Chile (Various publishers). 1881-93. 15v; Santiago de Chile, Prensas de la Universidad de Chile. 1930-35. 15v.

Coester, Alfred. The literary history of Spanish America. New York, Macmillan Co. 1916. p72, 197-203.

Crawford, W. Rex. A century of Latin-American thought. Cambridge, Harvard University Press. 1944. p52-7.

Henríquez Ureña, Pedro. Literary currents in Hispanic America. Cambridge, Harvard University Press. 1945. p94-111.

Lira Urquieta, Pedro. Andrés Bello. México, Buenos Aires, Fondo de Cultura Económica. 1948. 211p.

Mijares, Augusto. Hombres e ideas en América. Caracas, Escuela Técnica Industrial. 1940. p51-76.

Orrego Vicuña, Eugenio. Don Andrés Bello. Santiago de Chile, Prensas de la Universidad de Chile. 1935, 3d ed. 1940. 285p.

Torres-Ríoseco, Arturo. Epic of Latin American literature. New York, Oxford University Press. 1942. p44-85. Romantic upheaval in Spanish America.

EUCLIDES DA CUNHA (1866-1909)

AUTHOR OF OS SERTÕES

Many English readers suddenly "discovered" Euclides da Cunha when Samuel Putnam's translation of the Brazilian classic, *Os Sertões* appeared in English in 1944. Yet for over forty years it had been widely known by students of Latin American literature as the outstanding book of Brazil, or as one Brazilian critic puts it, "the work which best reflects our land and our people."[1] Stefan Zweig called it a "great national epic." Not only was it a great literary work in a new American and individual style, which marked, in 1902, Brazil's intellectual coming of age, but it was also a book which exercised a profound and formative influence on Brazilian thought concerning her national social problems, especially those of race and culture. It has been studied with profit by sociologists such as Gilberto Freyre, and has given rise to a stream of scientific and sociological study and to a school of regional novelists writing about northeast Brazil as well.

Cunha, writing an account of a military expedition sent to suppress an absurd but fanatically persistent rebellion in the backlands, led by the messianic Antonio Conselheiro, succeeded in turning the book into a keenly analytical and moving treatise of the geology, geography, climate, flora, fauna, and human life of the area. He managed to direct the attention of his countrymen to the national racial and social questions which the rebellion of Conselheiro brought into focus. The book was a violent cry of protest against the treatment of the semibarbarous people of the hinterland by the civilized people of the coast. It was a protest against militaristic violence. But it was also an eloquent plea for a higher degree of national cultural and spiritual unity in Brazil. It was this latter quality, perhaps, which gave it such a strong immediate appeal to Brazilians.

Cunha was born January 20, 1866, at Santa Rita do Rio Negro, in the old province of Rio de Janeiro. His mother, Donna Eudoxia Moreira da Cunha, died when he was three years old. Some writers have felt that the early death of his mother contributed to the development of his unusually complicated and tortured personality. From that time on he lived with relatives or at boarding schools. His father, Manuel Rodrigues Pimenta da Cunha, came from the province of Bahia, the province in which are located the Canudos backlands of which Cunha was later to write. Dom Manuel was a poet, and he apparently instilled in Euclides some of his own fondness for writing poetry, as well as seeing that he received a good education.

[1] Agrippino Grieco, quoted in Putnam's introduction to *Rebellion in the Backlands*. Chicago, University of Chicago Press. 1944. p iii.

His early schooling was divided between schools in Bahia and Rio de Janeiro, where he attended several *colégios*. At the Colégio Aquino, one of his teachers was the positivist Benjamin Constant, whose ideas contributed so much to the shaping of the republic of Brazil. With his schoolmates Cunha helped found a publication, *The Democrat (O democrata)* to which he contributed lyric poems. At the Colégio Aquino he absorbed the principles of positivism, and the ideas of Herbert Spencer, both so prevalent in Brazil on the eve of the republican revolution. He was greatly moved by Castro Alves' abolitionist poetry, and by Joaquim Nabuco's book on abolitionism. Like his fellow students he read Renan, Taine, Buckle, and Gobineau. Traces of Gobineau's theory of "superior" races may be seen later in his writing. In some way, during these years, he came into contact with the North American geographer, Orville Adelbert Derby, learned geology at the hands of John Casper Brenner, and something of archeology from Charles Frederick Hartt, leader of the Morgan expedition to Brazil.

In 1884 he entered the Polytechnic School and two years later the Military School, studying engineering. This phase of his life came to a sudden and dramatic end in 1888 when, in a mad fit of insubordination, he threw down his sword in the presence of the minister of war. This was during the last days of the empire, when republican sentiment was running high, and Cunha may simply have been carried away by youthful enthusiasm for the doctrinaire ideas of Benjamin Constant then popular in the army. Or his conduct may be explained as the first manifestation of a strong antimilitarism which characterized his later life. Needless to say, his career as a soldier was ended for the time being by this adolescent outburst. Only the intercession of his friends, and, possibly, that of the emperor, prevented its having more serious repercussions than dismissal from the army.

For a brief time he was in São Paulo, writing for a newspaper. Then after the proclamation of the Republic, and upon the plea of Benjamin Constant and some of his fellow students, he was reinstated in the Military School, in due course receiving a commission as a military engineer. He took an active part in defending the Republic against the counter-revolution of 1893, but his ingrained hostility to violence of all kinds again led him into trouble with the army authorities. A series of letters to a newspaper protesting against the death sentence imposed on the men who had bombed a republican journal brought him an assignment building army barracks in the provinces.

In 1896 he left the army to take up civil engineering. He was engaged on public works for the state of São Paulo when the Canudos "rebellion," led by a strange man who went by the name of Antonio Conselheiro, broke out in the backlands or *sertão* of Bahia in 1896. Cunha was sent by the newspaper *Estado de São Paulo* to report the results of the federal campaign against this strange group of rebels. His newspaper articles attracted some attention, but nothing like the sensation produced by the publication, five years later, of *Os Sertões* in which the story of this outlandish religious community and its terrifying and heroic resistance against the armed forces of the Republic was portrayed in its broader social, geographical, and psychological setting. So striking was the effect of this book on the Brazil of his day that the author was irrevocably identified with the subject of which he wrote, so that it is impossible today to think of Cunha without thinking of the half-crazy Antonio Conselheiro, and vice versa.

Antonio Vicente Mendes Maciel, who adopted the title of Antonio Conselheiro (Antonio Counselor), was descended from a numerous and respected but poor family of the back country of Ceará. Antonio had taken to the life of a wandering evangelist after a family tragedy in which his wife had run off with a police sergeant. He was a fanatic, probably a madman. With long hair and a disorderly matted beard, dressed in sandals, a rough, blue, canvas tunic, a hat with a broad brim turned down over his face, and carrying a pilgrim's staff, for over thirty years he wandered the backlands of Pernambuco, Sergipe and Bahia. He had acquired great ascendancy over the superstitious, mixed racial population that lived in the vast interior spaces of the Brazilian provinces, partly because of the asceticism of his life, partly because of his strange, mad eloquence. Almost inarticulate in normal conversation, he became a completely changed man when he began to preach. The wild and incoherent flood of language which then poured from his lips made the most striking effect imaginable on his audiences. Always distrusted by the regular clergy, he was tolerated by them for a long time as harmless. Eventually, however, he was denounced by the Bishop of Bahia. Meanwhile, he had been arrested and tried on what proved to be a false accusation that he had murdered his wife and his own mother. His release and reappearance in Bahia among his followers, on almost the exact day he had prophecied at the time of his arrest, was considered but another miracle among many already accredited to him, for the legend of the Conselheiro had grown to great proportions by this time.

He preached an extravagant millenarianism, the approaching end of the world, and urged his followers to give up all their possessions and all evidences of vanity in dress and conduct. Wherever he went he organized his disciples to repair churches, rebuild cemeteries, and to do other pious works. In 1886 he gathered some devotees around him in the village of Itapicurú, which he renamed *Bom Jesus* (Good Jesus). Driven from there by the Archbishop, he moved with his followers to an old abandoned cattle ranch at Canudos.

Canudos was in the midst of hard barren country on the river Vasa Barris, near the edge of the São Francisco valley. It had been a gold mining area a century before but was now given over to cowboys who gained a scanty living by tending, in the intervals between droughts, the herds owned by wealthy cattlemen living nearer the coast. *Jagunços* (ruffians), *sertanejos* (the cattle-tending inhabitants of the backlands), and a particularly large number of pious old women made up the settlement, sharing all things in common, in a kind of religious communism. The fifty ramshackle huts of the abandoned ranch quickly proved inadequate, and many more were added as new recruits and converts poured into the settlement. The total number of houses eventually reached over five thousand. Work of the community centered around building a huge church whose bell tower became the most striking landmark of the vicinity.

Maciel's refusal to permit the collection of government taxes brought on the conflict with federal authorities. A Capuchin friar was first sent to win over the rebels peacefully. This move failed, however because of the Conselheiro's fanatical opposition to the Church. Then in November 1896 a military expedition was dispatched. The savage resistance of the *jagunço* rebels was more than the military authorities had bargained for. Like the hard, arid land which produced them, they waged relentless war to the death. The first federal expedition was routed, as were two subsequent ones, until a fourth expedition of some six thousand men finally subdued Canudos by siege.

It was this last heroic resistance of the *sertanejos,* in which it required three months for the federal army to advance one hundred yards against a handful of backwoodsmen, which really moved Cunha to an appreciation of the deeper meaning of this seemingly minor military episode. It was not these fanatical followers of the Conselheiro who were to blame, after all. Their reactions were those of their harsh environment, the land and its recurrent floods and droughts, the religious fanaticism derived from Indian, Negro, and European sources, and from the isolation and cultural poverty of these hinterlands. Antonio Conselheiro was the expression of a new race which had emerged from the mixing of old racial elements. "In his behavior he reflected the obscure, formless aspirations of three races." In the *sertanejos* at Canudos Cunha saw "the very core of our nationality, the bedrock of our race."

The real fault, he said, lay with the civilized people of the coastal areas who had failed to bring education into the backlands. On this account the Canudos rebellion, small and isolated as it was, was a real trial for the Republic, since here the new government came up against something that was solid and substantial, sociologically, something American which opposed its progress. Interestingly enough, many Brazilian schoolbooks have come to adopt this thesis of Cunha that the Canudos rebellion was the most important civil conflict in the history of the Republic.

When *Os Sertões* appeared in 1902, the effect was electric. Years of careful thought and study had gone into writing this book, which had now become much more than the story of the Canudos campaign. Although it was written in the author's spare time, while he continued his work as a civil engineer, there was nothing casual or superficial about the book. It was a profound and thought-provoking study of Brazilian sociology and was hailed at once as a great work. Sixteen Portuguese editions followed in rapid succession, as well as editions in Spanish and English.

The author is by turns geologist, geographer, biologist, sociologist, and historian. The influence of positivist thought is evident in many places, in his strict biological determinism, for example, and in the determination with which he dwells on the close correspondence of the years of drought in the *Sertão* in the nineteenth century to those in the eighteenth century. In other ways, too, he was the victim of scientific preconceptions of his day, as his compatriot Gilberto Freyre has pointed out. Yet these are minor defects in a book which was at once recognized as great by critics in and out of Brazil.

Previous authors had written of the backlands, of course, and there was already in Brazil a *Sertanejo* school of fiction. But Cunha's book was something new and something more. Somehow he had managed to capture the significance of Antonio Conselheiro and the Canudos campaign. In this isolated backlands area, hewed out by a harsh and "angry" climate and topography he sensed, almost intuitively, the prime materials of which a united and great Brazil was to be formed. The injustice committed by the Republic at Canudos was now no longer simply an injustice against a small group of misguided religious fanatics. It was a crime against the national unity of the country. In the appearance of Maciel, the back country Messiah, he sensed a universal phenomenon of cultures in the process of creation. "In another milieu, under other conditions," writes the Brazilian critic José Verissimo, "Antonio Conselheiro is a Christ, a Mohammed, a Messiah, one of the many Mahdis, creators of religions in that fecund soil of human belief which is Asia."[2] It is sometimes difficult to determine whether the conflict of races and cultures, or the contact of man and the land in Brazil are uppermost in his thoughts. In any case, *Os Sertões*, while marking the literary coming of age of Brazil, as already noted, marked likewise a turning point in the evolution of Brazilian thought and letters, a turning to the land to extract from it that which was Brazilian and American.

Quiet and unobtrusive, Cunha was extremely sensitive and nervous in temperament. The strongest impulse of his nature was that against violence. He was also a democrat at heart, in spite of occasional utterances showing skepticism of the working of democracy in Brazil, comments quite typical of his class and of his day. He felt an intuitive sympathy for the Conselheiro and the *sertanejos*. Even his appearance was characteristic of a rebel against his class. He was disdainful of fine clothing and careless of his personal

[2] Quoted in Isaac Goldberg's *Brazilian Literature*. New York, Alfred A. Knopf. 1922. p220.

appearance. High cheek bones and hair which fell in a mass over his forehead suggested to more than one acquaintance the traits of an Indian. His contemporaries spoke of him as having a contemplative, absent-minded air. *Os Sertões* brought Cunha immediate national recognition as an author. In 1903 he was elected to the Brazilian Academy of Letters and the Institute of History. In the few remaining years of his life he produced several other books, while continuing work in his profession as a sanitary engineer, as surveyor of the Brazilian national boundaries, and as professor of logic in the Pedro II Institute. Yet none of his other achievements gained the importance of *Os Sertões*.

His life ended suddenly in tragedy when on August 15, 1909 he was shot down, probably by a personal enemy. The circumstances surrounding his death are somewhat obscure. He was supposedly working on a book which would make further exposures disagreeable to the army, and this explanation is given by some biographers as the cause of his death. It is more than likely, however, that a family scandal lay behind his murder.

He was only forty-three at the time, but into these brief years he had crowded many accomplishments as an engineer, journalist, and geographer. He had produced a book which marked the maturity of Brazilian national literature. In one of those rare books which capture the essence of a nation or of an age, he had sketched the lineaments of what might be called the sociological problem of Brazilian nationality.

Arciniegas, Germán. The green continent. New York, Alfred A. Knopf. 1944 p432-48.

Crawford, W. Rex. A century of Latin-American thought. Cambridge, Harvard University Press. 1944. 320p.

Cunninghame-Grahame, R. B. A Brazilian mystic. New York, Dial Press. 1926. 238p.

Cunha, Euclides da. Canudos: diario de uma expedição. (Coleção documentos brasileiros, 16). Rio de Janeiro, José Olympio. 1939. 186p.

Cunha, Euclides da. Rebellion in the backlands. (Tr. of Os Sertões by Samuel Putnam) Chicago, University of Chicago Press. 1944. 525p.

Freyre, Gilberto. Atualidade de Euclydes da Cunha. Rio de Janeiro, Casa do Estudante do Brasil. 1941. 59p.

Goldberg, Isaac. Brazilian literature. New York, Alfred A. Knopf. 1922. p210-21 and *passim*.

Pontes, Eloy. A vida dramatica de Euclydes da Cunha. (Coleção documentos brasileiros, 13) Rio de Janeiro, José Olympio. 1938. 342p.

Werneck Sodré, Nelson. Historia da literatura brasileira. Rio de Janeiro, José Olympio. 2d ed. rev. 1940. p209-12.

Zweig, Stefan. Brazil, land of the future. New York. Viking Press. 1942. p 158-160.

RUBÉN DARÍO (1867-1916)

POET

One of the strongest first impressions of a North American making the acquaintance of Latin American life is that very great importance is attached to poets and poetry. Is this addiction of the normal Latin American to poetry a Latin inheritance, an Indian inheritance, or one derived in part from the Negro delight in poetry and song? To what extent does it reflect the society and culture of a class stratified society which, with a few notable exceptions, is still largely agrarian? All these factors have doubtless exercised some influence, and the question is too complicated to be dealt with here at any length. It is enough, now, to note that this widespread poetic interest can be observed in the most casual reading of Latin American newspapers and books. Those readers who have enjoyed the privilege of a Latin American evening devoted to reading poetry will have had it brought home to them more forcefully in an experience never to be forgotten. It is a commonplace, though an important one, that any civilization is much more fully understood if viewed with the intimate understanding of its poets. This is true of Latin America to a special degree. For there poets and poetry enjoy genuine prestige. It was a Uruguayan poet who wrote:

Oh Poesía!
Quien te niegue, arderá en el infierno.[1]

(Oh Poetry!
Whoever denies thee will burn in Hell.)

The poet-statesman, moreover, is a frequent Latin American type. One of the greatest was the Cuban revolutionary leader, José Martí. Rubén Darío, although he did not win great fame as a statesman conforms to this type. A great deal of his life was spent as a diplomat. But his influence as the greatest poet of his age in Spanish America was exercised even more significantly in shaping the mind and spirit of a whole generation of Latin Americans.

The political content and significance of his writing is small, of course, and the first reaction of the reader at finding him included in a book on leaders of thought and action who have shaped the course of Latin American democracy may well be one of surprise. His Hispanic Americanism and his almost aristocratic disdain for the commonplace might indeed even suggest some of the elements of social reactionary spirit. But Darío was

[1] Figueira. Gastón. *Acordeón Marinero*. Montevideo, 1945. p 19.

far from being a reactionary. Quite the contrary, he played an important and constructive role in building the complex of attitudes, ideas, and values which form an important part of twentieth-century life in Latin America. The spirit of his rebellion, on the whole, seems more American than European, as does the "bumptiousness" which went with it. His ideas and the example of his bouyant spirit contributed greatly to the youth movement of the early years of this century which was forming a new Latin American spirit of self-confidence and spiritual freedom, free from the colonialism of the past as well as from the frustration produced by the nineteenth century revolutions and general political instability.

Felix Rubén García Sarmiento was born in the little town of Metapa in Nicaragua in 1867, the year in which a treaty was concluded between Nicaragua and the United States providing for the construction of an interoceanic canal across Nicaragua. The name Darío was one he adopted later, perhaps because of its sonorous, poetic sound, or perhaps simply because Darío was the name of a locally famous ancestor for whom all the family were popularly called. His parents separated shortly after Rubén's birth and he was brought up in León by his maternal relatives, the Ramírez family. A precocious child, he learned to read at the age of three, wrote verses at the age of five or six, and by the time he was twelve was known as "the boy poet" throughout Central America. By the time he was fourteen he had already run into difficulty by writing for an opposition political journal, *La verdad*, and acquired a local reputation for his knowledge of Masonic lore. In this period he taught grammar in a secondary school in León while continuing his own studies.

From his autobiography we know that he had read *Don Quijote*, the *Thousand and One Nights*, the Bible, Cicero, Mme. de Staël, Moratín, and the classic Spanish plays. Through the influence of friends he had received a position in the National Library at Managua, where his reading broadened to include all the Spanish classical authors. At this early period he seems to have acquired his first ideas of rejuvenating the language and form of Spanish poetry.

But he was equally precocious in love. When at the age of fourteen he announced his serious intention to marry "a green-eyed, chestnut-haired maiden of a gentle pallor" he was packed off by friends and relatives to neighboring El Salvador. Here he came under the inspiring influence of the great literary master and poet, Francisco Gavidia, and a circle of the latter's friends who were already experimenting with the ideas of the French Modernists in Spanish verse and prose. Gavidia, particularly, introduced him to the works of Victor Hugo and to that poet's innovations in poetic meter.

He soon returned to Nicaragua, but love affairs were to torture his life constantly, and it may have been another romantic disappointment which soon caused him to leave again, this time for Chile. The next two and a half years were spent in Valparaiso, where he wrote for several newspapers and was employed part of the time in the customs house.

It was in Valparaiso that he published, with the help of some friends, the book of poems and prose-poems which won him worldwide acclaim, *Azul*. It was not his greatest literary work, but it was the book which brought him immediate recognition as a great master of Spanish language and verse, and made him at once the acknowledged leader of the modernist tendency in Latin America. Blue to Darío was the color of dreams and of art—a symbol of the new literary movement. In "El Rey Burgués," one of the prose tales in *Azul*, a stranger addressing the King of the Commonplace says:

> I have caressed great nature, and I have sought the warmth of the ideal, the verse that is in the stars, in the depths of the sky, in the pearl, in the profundities of the ocean, I have tried to forge ahead! For the time of great revolutions is approaching, with a Messiah all light, all striving and power, and his spirit must be received with strophes of steel, strophes of gold, strophes of love. . .[2]

Darío acknowledged that he owed much to contemporary French poets, especially Gautier and Catulle Mendès. But he was not an imitator, and cannot be identified with any of the "schools" of the day. He was not a Parnassian, nor a Symbolist nor a "decadent." He put himself at the head of a revolt from the sterile academic traditions of romanticism and pseudo-classicism which had ruled Latin American literature and had prevented free literary expression. Like Gavidia and his friends, Darío struck out boldly for an American literary expression which would be at the same time cosmopolitan. The tendencies which he initiated had the widest implications and consequences. They were to produce not only a new literature, an American literature, but one with revolutionary and sometimes almost messianic trends which have brought about the distinctive flavor of present-day Latin American literature.

Darío returned to his native Nicaragua in 1889, already a famous poet. In 1892 he was appointed to represent his country in Spain at the celebration marking the four hundredth anniversary of the discovery of America. On his return from this diplomatic mission he visited the great ex-president of Colombia, Rafael Nuñez, who secured his appointment as Colombian consul in Buenos Aires.

Before going to Buenos Aires he made a tour of the United States and Europe in 1893. In the United States he met José Martí and the group of Cubans who were preparing the movement for Cuban independence. And in France he made the acquaintance of Paul Verlaine and other French writers.

[2] Translation taken from Isaac Goldberg's *Studies in Spanish-American Literature*. New York, Brentano's. 1920. p 131.

He took the literary youth of Argentina by storm. Sergio Bagú has written of how Darío's revolutionary idealism and his bohemianism stirred the minds of José Ingenieros and his followers in the late years of the 1890's. His *Prosas profanas* is of this period and is considered by one critic his best from the standpoint of form. It also represents a more complete break than *Azul* with the romanticism of the past. The sonnet "To Margarita," "La Sonatina," and the "Colloquy of the Centaurs," all in this volume, rank among his best known pieces. During this stay in Buenos Aires he also published *Los raros* (Rare Spirits). These were impressions of eminent persons of the times, and were, for the most part, published originally in the newspaper *La nación*.

It was as a correspondent of *La nación* that Darío went to Spain, in 1898, after the outbreak of the Spanish-American War. Most of the rest of his life was spent in Spain and France. In Spain his arrival initiated the movement of literary Hispanic-Americanism, which was so vitally related to the regeneration of Spanish poetry and letters. One of the outstanding Spanish poets of the day, Martínez Sierra, has acknowledged Spain's debt to Darío in unforgettable words:

> España corazón tiene esa deuda de cariño para el poeta americano, como España juventud e intelecto tiene la de ciencia y belleza para el poeta universal. Así, amorosamente, debemos pagar nuestra admiración con palabras enseñadas a nosotros por él, en ritmos aprendidos al sonar de su flauta. . .

> (The heart of Spain owes a debt of affection to the American poet just as Spanish youth and intellect owes one of knowledge of science and beauty to the universal poet. Thus, with love, we must pay our admiration in words taught us by him, in rhythms learned to the sound of his flute. . .)[3]

His articles in *La nación* during the years following the War of 1898 are considered by the Spanish historian Rafael Altamira as one of the early indications of Hispanic-Americanism coming from America. The roots of the movement, of course, go back to the scientific congresses held in 1892, which, it will be recalled, Darío had attended. This new literary Hispanic-Americanism was frequently characterized by an antagonism toward the United States, the "Colossus of the North," whose great expansion of power had been shown in the war with Spain, an expansion, it was felt, which threatened the very existence of Latin America. In this spirit Darío composed, not his best poem, but certainly the one which is best known in North America, *To Roosevelt*:

> It is with the voice of the Bible, or the verse of Walt Whitman,
> that one should approach you, hunter!
> Primitive and modern, simple yet complex,
> With somewhat of Washington and more of Nimrod!

[3] Quoted from his *Motivos* by John E. Englekirk in *El hispanoamericanismo y la generación del 98.* 31 p. (Reprinted from *Revista iberoamericana*. 2:1-31. November 1940) Translation by author.

You are the United States,
you are the future invader
of that ingenuous America in whom glows indigenous blood,
and which still prays to Jesus Christ and speaks Spanish.

You are a proud and powerful exemplar of your race;
You are cultured, skilful; you oppose Tolstoi.
And dominating horses, or assassinating tigers,
You are an Alexander-Nebuchadnezzar.
(You are a professor of energy
as today's madmen declare.)
You believe that life is a conflagration,
that progress is an eruption;
that wherever you send the bullet,
You implant the future.

                    No.

The United States are powerful and great.
When they shudder there is a deep trembling
That passes along the enormous vetebrae of the Andes.
When you cry there comes the roar of the lion.
Hugo told it to Grant: "The stars are yours."
(There scarcely shines, as it rises, the Argentine sun,
and the star of Chile surges forth. . .) You are rich.
To the cult of Hercules you join the cult of Mammon;
and lighting the way of facile conquest,
Liberty raises its torch before New York.

The poem concludes with a clarion call to the America of Montezuma,
the Inca and Columbus, Catholic and Spanish America—the "thousand cubs
of the Spanish Lion":

Se necesitaría, Roosevelt, ser por Dios mismo,
el Riflero terrible y el fuerte Cazador,
para poder tenernos en vuestras férreas garras.
Y, pues contaís con todo, falta una cosa: Dios!

('Tis need, O Roosevelt, that you be God himself. . .
Before you hold us fast in your grasping iron claws.
And though you count on all, one thing is lacking,—God.)[4]

No other Latin American, except possibly the Argentine Ugarte, gave
stronger literary expression to this deep-lying Hispanic-American suspicion
and distrust of the United States.   And like some others, Darío was later
to regret the venom of his pen.   It was largely repudiated in a subsequent
poem *Salutación al Águila*, written to welcome the North American delegates to the Pan American Conference in Brazil in 1906.   Yet apparently

[4] The English translation, except that of the last four lines of the poem, is from Isaac Goldberg's *Studies in Spanish-American Literature*. New York, Brentano's. 1920. p 158. The original may be found in *Cantos de vida y esperanza*. (*Obras completas*, v7) Madrid, Editorial
Mundo Latino. 1920. The E. C. Hills translation of the last four lines is from Alfred Coester's
Literary History of Spanish-America. New York, Macmillan Co. 1916. p464-5.

it still prevented his serving as Envoy Extraordinary to the Mexican government for the centenary of Mexican independence in 1910.

The lesson of this terrible ode to the first Roosevelt should not be lightly dismissed, even though Darío grossly underestimated the forces of restraint and responsibility in the North American political system. For dangerous and irresponsible forces in the United States were thinking of the very kind of economic, political, and spiritual domination which tore this protest of hate and fear from his heart and pen. And his violent diatribe was not without influence in strengthening the determination of those forces of liberalism in the United States whose wisdom was ultimately to restrain the grosser tendencies of expansionism.

His personal life was tragic. The inner freedom which his poetry expressed so admirably he was unable to achieve in his own life. Addicted to drinking and to the use of morphine, he wrote many of his best poems in brief lucid spells between periods of complete surrender to drunkenness. His first wife, Rafaela Contreras, had died during his visit to Madrid for the Columbus Celebration in 1892. Shortly afterward he married Rosaria Murillo under unfortunate and mysterious circumstances. The marriage was certainly a failure. Not his wife, but another, Francisca Sánchez, a kind-hearted but uneducated Spanish woman and the faithful companion of his later years, cared for him like a child during his long periods of melancholy and morbid fear.

Perhaps ill health lay at the root of much of Darío's irregular and bohemian way of life. At all events he was a fatally sick man when he made his last return to America in 1915. He had undertaken a lecture tour which took him to New York, Rio de Janeiro and Colombia, but illness forced him to give up the tour and he "returned to Nicaragua to die," as he himself explained. Here death found him early in 1916 after a few months of troubled illness.

This sick and troubled soul, in the brief span of life accorded him, had exercised an almost unbelievable influence on the mind and heart of the Spanish speaking world. Isaac Goldberg has observed that his personality was "compounded of childish fears, spiritual doubts, pagan propensities and eternal preoccupation with the eternal feminine." [5] His life displays all these weaknesses. Yet for a quarter of a century his poetry had pointed the way to a new freedom and vigor for the mind of Latin America and Spain in its search for a rebirth. Out of his own morbid fear and timidity he had somehow distilled a new confidence, aptly expressed in two lines from his Slings, as translated by Alice Stone Blackwell:

> Wounded, Goliath's soul has fled.
> I come to Thee, from out the sky:
> Lo, David's radiant soul am I.[6]

[5] Quoted in Alice Stone Blackwell's *Some Spanish American Poets*. Philadelphia, University of Pennsylvania Press. 1937. p539.
[6] *Ibid.* p189-90.

Blackwell, Alice Stone. Some Spanish-American poets. Philadelphia, University of Pennsylvania Press. 1937. p182-202.

Coester, Alfred. Literary history of Spanish America. New York, Macmillan Co. 1916. p457-466.

Contreras, Francisco. Rubén Darío, su vida y su obra. Santiago de Chile, Ercilla. 1937. 364p.

Daireaux, Max. Panorama de la littérature hispano-américaine. Paris, Kra. 1930. p95-106.

Darío, Rubén. Obras completas. Madrid, Mundo Latino. 1916-24. 25v.

Darío, Rubén. La vida de Rubén Darío, escrita por el mismo. Barcelona, Maucci. 1916. 287p. (In Obras completas)

Doyle, Henry Grattan. Bibliography of Rubén Darío (1867-1916). Cambridge, Harvard University Press. 1935. 28p.

Englekirk, John E. El hispanoamericanismo y la generación del 98. 31p. (Reprinted from Revista iberoamericana. 2:1-31. November 1940)

Goldberg, Isaac. Studies in Spanish-American literature. New York, Brentano's. 1920. 377p. Ch. II.

Melián Lafinur, Álvaro. Figuras americanas. Paris, Franco-Ibero-Americana. 1926. p167-191.

Watt, Stewart and Peterson, H. F. Builders of America. New York, Harper & Bros. 1942. p258-68.

JOSÉ ENRIQUE RODÓ (1871-1917)

ARIEL

It was peculiarly appropriate that turbulent, revolution-ridden Uruguay should produce the fine, quiet, and serene voice of Rodó at the end of the nineteenth century. Yet, at first thought, as critics have remarked, the appearance of a figure like Rodó in Uruguay at this time seems a great enigma. Nowhere else in Latin America had democratic idealism seemed less successful, up to this time, in the struggle with the stultifying forces of selfish personalism thriving in the complicated politics of a buffer state. But Uruguay, by 1900, was already stirring with indications of the political and economic transformation which was soon to place her in the vanguard of progressive American nations. To be sure, when Rodó's *Ariel* appeared in that year it would have taken a great prophet indeed to see in the politics of the Oriental republic the outlines of these changes to come. But *Ariel* was all the more effective because of this marked contrast with the background from which it sprang. The voice of *Ariel* was the annunciation of the spirit which was to animate not only the new Uruguay, but a new Latin America. Although it was destined to have little direct effect on politics it was, indirectly, even more significant and effective because its quiet tone of spiritual abnegation and heroism was so clear a challenge to the factionalism and personalism which ruled Uruguayan political life.

Rodó was probably the least American, and the most universal, of the modern Latin American writers. He was keenly sensitive to the conflicts and problems of the protean struggle involved in the rapid development of life and culture in America, particularly in his own southern South America, where the invasion of European immigration was visibly transforming the simple herding economy into a rich, urban-centered, commercial society of large-scale production for export. He did not deny the American scene, nor its amorphous democracy. Yet neither did the basis of his thought spring from the American soil or the stresses and strains of American life. It flowed rather, as from a deep well, tapping basic Hellenic and Christian sources of the patterns of Western culture.

Although his most productive years, from 1909 to 1917, corresponded closely to those of the crusade for political and economic reform led by José Batlle and his enthusiastic band of young followers, Rodó remained largely aloof from the tumult of this successful struggle for constitutional reform. His writing was his life, and his bibliography is the major part of his biography. Even his biographers write little of his personal life.

He was born in Montevideo, of a good family, and this family background inevitably caused him to reflect something of the sensitiveness of his class toward the challenge presented by the overwhelming wave of European immigration and the changes it was bringing. Educated, likewise, in Montevideo, he lived his professional life as a journalist there, never leaving America until the first World War, when a brief journalistic excursion to Europe brought illness and death in Italy at the early age of forty-six. Twice a member of parliament, and briefly a professor of literature, he seems to have been ill-adapted for success in either. Wearing thick glasses which betrayed his nearsightedness, timid in any social gathering, he was cold, shy, ill-at-ease. The confidence of the detached Olympian tone of his writing was probably a psychological compensation for this morbid timidity. At any rate his pen speaks with assurance and the sustained optimism for which a generation of Latin American youth was avid—a generation unnerved by the many failures of Latin American democracy, and troubled by the rapid tempo of social and economic change and especially by the apparent threat to their cultural, economic, and even political autonomy posed by the expansion of Anglo-American industrial and political power.

The weakness of Rodó lay in this dispassionate aloofness. He urged passionate dedication to action at the highest idealistic level, and his appeal to the idealism of youth made him, with José Ingenieros of Argentina, one of the two great idols of the universities. But, unlike Ingenieros, while he urged action, his fundamental estheticism kept him on the sidelines, a contemplative observer. In his discerning recognition of the moral basis of education for leadership he was the Thomas Arnold of Spanish America; but his influence failed to produce the moral incentive to vigorous political leadership which Arnold gave to British education. Largely sterile in the political and economic fields, it found its best expression and greatest influence in literature and art.

The basis of his thought was an idealistic revolt against the growing materialism of his times, and its tendency to stifle the life of the spirit upon which all real cultural achievement is dependent. He believed that "when democracy does not heighten its spirit by the influence of a strong idealistic preoccupation, which shares its rule with that of preoccupation with material interests, it leads fatally to the poverty of mediocrity. . . ." [1] Alberdi's famous aphorism, *gobernar es poblar* (to govern is to populate), he points out, was a natural statement to issue from a leader and a nation faced with the problems of peopling vast areas. But such a quantitative formula he felt to be a wholly inadequate statement of the objectives of a society. *Ariel*, the blithe spirit of Shakespeare's *The Tempest*, around which Rodó's most influential book was written, represents idealism, order, noble inspira-

[1] *Ariel.* Quoted by Emilio Oribe in *El pensamiento vivo de Rodó,* Buenos Aires, Losada. 1944. p41.

tion, good taste, and heroism. It is the highest reason and the finest sentiment.

Few Latin Americans so thoroughly reflected the French thought and culture which were molding the Latin America of his day. Renan was his favorite, but his wide reading and eclectic taste led him to such diverse sources as Taine, De Tocqueville, Carlyle, Emerson, Flaubert, Ibsen, Nietzsche, Sarmiento, Martí, and Montalvo. Following the tendencies of Renan he drew deeply on classical thought. To the hierarchical structure of classicism he added the vital moral force of romantic individualism, absorbed from the spirit of the nineteenth century. Thus, in some respects, he presaged the later cult of Dilthey and Bergson in Latin America.

From Christianity he derived one of the two basic historical impulses which give contemporary civilization its essential characteristics: the sentiment of equality. But Christian equality, he felt, was vitiated by a certain ascetic depreciation of spiritual and cultural selection. The second basic impulse he saw coming from classical civilization—a sense of order and hierarchy, and religious respect for genius. But this, likewise, was vitiated by an "aristocratic disdain" for the humble and the weak. Indeed, too many Latin American intellectuals of Rodó's day showed this "aristocratic disdain" for the market place and the turbulence of politics. Always sensitive to the gulf which separated them from the illiterate poverty-stricken masses of their countrymen, they had lost, to a large extent, the confidence in democracy which characterized their predecessors of the nineteenth century, and had come to regard democracy as a spurious shield for crass materialism and demagogy. Rodó revolted against the materialism which, in the form of a monotonous panegyric of all things American, had become so annoying to the intellectuals of his day. But he was also the annunciator of a new note of confident intellectual leadership of democratic forces.

Democracy, in its striving for material success, he pointed out, was laying the necessary basis for the finest spiritual and cultural achievement. Democracy and science, he said, are the two "irreplaceable supports" of our civilization. But the definitive triumph of democracy could come only through a synthesis of the two basic historical factors which shaped modern life, that is, through a synthesis of Judaic Christianity and Hellenism, the classical spirit of hierarchy. And both of these historical elements were in their essence systems of freedom. The essence of both, their central element, was the spirit of *Ariel*, the immortal protagonist, whose supreme law was escape from material and earthly ties.

The appearance of *Ariel* in 1900 was a milestone in the life of the American spirit and in American letters. Undoubtedly much of its success and influence was due to the classic excellence of its Spanish prose. But of equal importance, certainly, was its quiet, firmly serene, and stoic-like affirmation of spiritual purpose and values which could be achieved within a democratic American setting. The scene is the study of the revered master, Prospero, bidding farewell to his students gathered around a bronze statue of *Ariel*. The measured discourse of the master, oracular and aphoristic, deals with the most serious problems of the life of the spirit. Here Rodó gives best expression to his fundamental thesis of a fusion of Hellenism and Christianity, and makes his most eloquent appeal to youth to follow a course of abnegation and sacred consecration to the "unknown future." Throughout, the book breathes a high sense of the role of spirit and ideas. "Men and peoples work . . . under the inspiration of ideas as irrational beings under the inspiration of instincts."

With Renan, Rodó believed that democracy, in its leveling tendency, tends to mediocrity. But he refused to follow Renan in condemnation of the basic democratic principle of equality of rights. Democracy, says the master, must be balanced by recognition of the need for a spiritual elite. But "the spirit of democracy is . . . for our civilization, a principle of life against which it is useless to rebel." In such widely divergent sources as Taine, Renan, Carlyle, Flaubert, Ibsen, Nietzsche, and Emerson (a voice from the most positivist of the democracies) the master finds recognition of this intellectual and spiritual need. Science, too, speaks of the necessity of selection. But it is in art that "the sense of the select" finds its most natural medium. Here, "with deep resonance, the notes which acknowledge the sentiment . . . of the spirit vibrate." He was keenly sensitive to the current Parnassian spirit of decadence, and aware that his words might be taken to suggest taking refuge from the present in the past in order to hear these voices of the spirit in art. So his warning is strong against "the delicate and sickly Parnassianism" to which an "aristocratic disdain for the present" leads. In his last words Prospero calls on American youth to renew its ideals and hopes by dedication to the spirit of *Ariel*. He dreams of the day when American achievements will show that "the Cordillera which rises on the soil of America has been carved out as the definitive pedestal of this statue [Ariel], to be the immutable altar for its veneration."

No other book by Rodó approaches *Ariel* in importance. *The Motives of Proteus*, published in 1909, was a collection of brief essays, elaborating many of the ideas of Ariel, and centering around the concept of *becoming*, the ideal of life. In it he urged Latin Americans to devote themselves to that increased specialization in their vocations required by advancing civilization, and, by cultivating their potentialities to the fullest, to develop not only their own personalities but the larger personality of Latin American society as well.[2] His essay on Montalvo,[3] in its concern with the Indian, was his nearest approach to dealing with the basic social problems of Amer-

[2] See W. Rex Crawford, *A Century of Latin-American Thought*. Cambridge, Harvard University Press. 1944. Ch.IV.
[3] In his *Hombres de América*. Barcelona, Cervantes. 1920. 255p.

ica. His *Mirror of Prospero* (1913), a collection of speeches, articles and criticisms, however, contains one of the finest statements of the American ideal of internationalism to be found anywhere:

> I have always believed that in our America it was not possible to speak of many fatherlands, but rather of one great, single country; I have always believed that in America, more than anywhere else, it behooves us, without destroying this idea of a fatherland, to make it greater and wider and purify it of all that is narrow and negative . . . and raise above the idea of the nation, the idea of America.[4]

The final evaluation of Rodó and his contribution to American and democratic thought, is still a matter of profound difference of opinion, and he has become in Spanish America the symbol of an attitude to be accepted or rejected. He has been criticized severely by Americanists such as Luis Alberto Sánchez of Peru and Alberto Zum Felde of Uruguay, who consider him an esthete, lacking in psychological and sociological understanding. They see in his search for spiritual superiority chiefly a justification for the technical backwardness of Latin America.[5] The Argentine Emilio Oribe, on the other hand, while admitting that Rodó expressed the unrest of a Latin America confronted with the great practical achievements of North America, insists that his universal humanistic spirit set the "paradigm" of future American thought, announcing "a series of the greatest accomplishments to come which it will be necessary for America to fulfill that she may be worthy of the thought of the world."[6]

Certainly Rodó's cool, aloof path to moral and spiritual excellence and leadership, through fusion of the classical and Christian ideals, is a difficult one to follow, with a peculiar attraction, however, for the esthete. His criticism of the Parnassianism of his day, and his frank acceptance of science and democracy, always couched in the finest Spanish prose, were an important and necessary correction to the over-fastidious, class conscious literary circles of his day. In a day when other literary leaders like Francisco García Calderón and Leopoldo Lugones were compromising with the principle of dictatorship, Rodó stood firmly for liberty. But his influence led all too easily to a merely contemplative attitude toward the pressing social problems of the democratic Latin America which was struggling into existence, however clearly he may have seen this society in its process of "becoming." On the other hand it would be premature, and probably unjust, to underestimate his contribution to the growth of humanistic democratic thought in the American scene, or the long-range importance of that tendency in the development of Latin American society and culture. Final judgment of Rodó will depend upon final judgment of this tendency he repre-

---

[4] *El mirador de Prospero*. Quoted in W. Rex Crawford, op. cit. p88.
[5] See Luis Alberto Sánchez, *Balance y liquidación del novecientos*. Santiago de Chile, Ercilla. 1941. p71-88. See also Alberto Zum Felde, *Proceso intelectual del Uruguay*. Montevideo, Claridad. 1941. p236.
[6] Oribe, Emilio. *Op. cit.* p36.

sents. His influence, waning for a time under the attacks of contemporary liberal leaders like Sánchez and Zum Felde, may be currently reviving. On the whole, however, it seems fair to say that from the standpoint of today his most lasting contribution to democratic thought seems to have been literary and esthetic rather than social in the fullest sense of that term.

Crawford, W. Rex. A century of Latin-American thought. Cambridge, Harvard University Press. 1944. p79-90.

Henríquez Ureña, Max. Rodó y Rubén Darío. Habana, Sociedad Editorial Cuba Contemporánea. 1918. 152p.

Melián Lafinur, Álvaro. Figuras americanas. Paris, Franco-Ibero-Americana. 1926. p131-140.

Oribe, Emilio. El pensamiento vivo de Rodó. (Biblioteca del pensamiento vivo, 30) Buenos Aires, Losada. 1944. 222p.

Pérez Petit, Victor. Rodó: su vida—su obra. Montevideo, García. 1918. 512p.

Sánchez, Luis Alberto. Balance y liquidación de novecientos. Santiago de Chile, Ercilla. 1941. p71-88.

Zaldumbide, Gonzálo. Montalvo y Rodó. New York, Instituto de las Españas en los Estados Unidos. 1938. 282p.

Zum Felde, Alberto. Proceso intelectual del Uruguay. Montevideo, Claridad. 1941. 639p.

JOSÉ INGENIEROS (1877-1925)

LEADER OF ARGENTINE YOUTH

Even more than the United States, Argentina is an immigrant nation, in the sense of a country basically transformed by the large stream of immigration which it received in the late nineteenth and early twentieth centuries. The chief source of this immigration was Spain, but Italy came a close second. Italian immigrants swelled the rapidly growing ranks of agricultural and industrial workers. They also furnished their share of the intellectual, social, and cultural leadership of Argentina's rapidly expanding urban centers, helping to give them a quality of cosmopolitanism equaled only in neighboring Uruguay. The career of José Ingenieros was typical of these times and tendencies. Son of an obscure Italian immigrant labor leader and journalist, he grew up with the new Argentina to become one of the best spokesmen of its progressive tendencies, as well as the most influential leader of that generation of its youth.

With Rodó he shared the distinction of being the Spanish American author most widely read by Latin American students, and with his contemporary, Alejandro Korn, shared the intellectual peerage of the Argentina of his day. Yet neither Rodó nor Korn, nor indeed any other figure of Latin American thought and letters during the first quarter of this century, approached Ingenieros in the impact which he made on the mind of his times, or in the vigor and originality with which he applied himself to the solution of immediate and long-range social and scientific problems of the day. In this sense he was without peer as the master of the generation of social and political leadership, youthful then, which, now mature, guides the destiny of Latin America.

He was born April 24, 1877, in Buenos Aires. Salvador Ingenieros and Ana Tagliava, his parents, were recent immigrants from Italy. Salvador Ingenieros had been a member of workers' organizations in Italy, a member of the First International, and an active member of the Masonic lodges in which much of the Italian revolutionary and reform agitation centered. For several decades he edited the *Revista masónica (Masonic Review)* in Buenos Aires, making of it a center of contact with European ideas. José thus grew up in a socialist and liberal environment. His father took great interest in his son's intellectual development, setting him at an early age to the correction of proofs and to the translation of French, Italian, and English books.

For his early education he was sent to the Instituto Nacional of Pedro Ricaldoni, and to the Colegio Catedral al Norte of Pablo Pizzurno. In 1888 he entered the Colegio Nacional of Buenos Aires. Here he was a serious and ambitious student, but his interests were greatly influenced by the revolutionary disturbances and strikes which marked the early 1890's in Argentina. In 1892, while completing his baccalaureate, he headed a student strike, editing a paper, *La reforma*, for that purpose.

In 1893, at the age of sixteen, Ingenieros entered the university. The breadth of his interests at this time appears in his enrolling for both the law course and that in medicine. This double interest was also characteristic of the strong counter-pulls of detached scientific interest and concern for public questions which his whole career shows so clearly. He was an enthusiastic student and an omnivorous reader, but this did not prevent him from being quickly initiated into the activities of the growing socialist movement among the university students. In 1894 he helped organize a University Socialist Center in the Hospital de Clínicas, and in 1895 he became secretary of the Argentine Socialist Workers' Party, organized in that year by Professor Juan B. Justo of the faculty of medicine. The same year he published an eighty-eight page pamphlet, *What Is Socialism?* for the University Socialist Center. Sold at a low price, it received wide attention, and was his first important published work. In 1896, at the age of eighteen, he was nominated for congress by the Socialist Party, but withdrew in favor of an older candidate.

The years from 1895 to 1898 were, for Ingenieros, years of widening interests and a wide variety of activities. Political agitation occupied too large a part of his time and seriously detracted from his medical studies. He read widely: Loria, Tarde, Spencer, and de Greef in social sciences; Ibsen, Tolstoy, Zola, and Nietzsche in literature. Rubén Darío came to Buenos Aires in 1897 and stayed for two years. His *Azul*, recently published, made the Nicaraguan poet the rising star of Spanish literature. Ingenieros was one of the leading spirits in the group experiencing the stimulus of Darío's revolutionary ideas and spirit. This group of young intellectuals of the recently established Ateneo de Juventud became the center of the new Argentine literary tendencies. With Darío's support, Ingenerios, the poet Leopoldo Lugones, and several other young Argentine writers started a bi-weekly literary journal, *La montaña*, which was to be avowedly revolutionary and socialist. The violence of Ingenieros' article, "The Bourgeois Reptiles," published in the third issue, brought his arrest and sequestration of the issue. He was sentenced to pay a fine of three hundred pesos or serve five months in prison, but the sentence was never imposed. The paper continued for twelve issues, however, until constant deficits brought it to an end. In addition to his inflammatory articles, Ingenieros contributed critical articles such as "Pablo Groussac and Socialism" and numerous book reviews. The group of young writers gravitated then to *El mercurio*, which continued to reflect Darío's modernist tendencies.

This literary activity and constant agitation developed his talents for writing and speaking, and had made him already a writer of note in his native city. He read broadly in sociology and psychology. But his medical studies suffered, and in December 1898, he failed one of his medical examinations. The next year proved to be a turning point in his life and career. Already he had come under the influence of José María Ramos Mejía, professor of the medical school in charge of the clinic dealing with nervous diseases, and also Director of the National Department of Hygiene. In 1899 Ingenieros found in Francisco de Veyga, professor of legal medicine, an even stronger influence. It was Veyga who helped him to end at last the conflict of interests of the preceding years. After 1899 he abandoned his militant agitation and turned more seriously to scientific work.

Ramos Mejía made Ingenieros head of his clinic. Francisco de Veyga guided his studies in anthropological and other aspects of criminology, and made him his collaborator in the publication of the medical journal, *La semana médica*. By the time he had completed his medical studies in the university, Ingenieros had developed well defined scientific interests in criminology, abnormal psychology, and psychiatry. From 1904 to 1911 he was director of psychiatric observation for the police department in Buenos Aires. From 1902 to 1913 he published a review, *Archives of Criminology, Legal Medicine and Psychiatry*, which brought together the writings of the most distinguished scientists in these fields writing in Spanish, and contributed enormously to the development of scientific interests in these important subjects in Argentina. His fame had already extended to Europe before 1905, when he was sent to Rome to attend the International Congress of Psychology. There he made so great an impression that he was invited by the Italian psychologist Enrico Morselli, to stay in Europe as his assistant.

On his return from Europe he persuaded Joaquín V. González to establish at the University of La Plata an Institute of Criminology, of which Ingenieros was named director. When Veyga resigned from the faculty of medicine in 1911 Ingenieros applied for the chair of legal medicine, but political influences apparently prevented his appointment, although his application was supported by a bibliography of hundreds of items in at least five languages. Keenly disappointed, he set out again for Europe, where he stayed for several years.

The Argentina to which he returned in 1915, in the midst of the first World War, was one of ferment and rapid change. The war had brought national prosperity, and with it a much stronger sense of Argentine nationalism, reflected in her determined neutrality. Confidence in the national future ran strong. The Radical Party, the party of liberal reform, was challenging the traditional political leadership of the landowners and *caudillos*. The electoral system had been reformed and the Radical Party was to win its first national election the next year.

Immediately following his return he founded the *Revista de filosofía,* which became the chief center of his work and influence during the rest of his life. Since 1908 his attention had been turning from criminology to the broader interests of psychology and sociology. Failure to secure the coveted appointment to the faculty of medicine at this time may have influenced somewhat this change of interests. At any rate, from 1915, until his death in 1925, Ingenieros made the *Revista de filosofía* the center of a great effort to impress scientific principles and methods upon all aspects of Argentine intellectual life. Articles on biology, psychology, and sociology rubbed elbows with others on educational reform, philosophy, and history. Through its pages Ingenieros spoke as the acknowledged leader of positive or scientific thought in Latin America.

The mere bulk of his publications is impressive. The definitive edition of his works consists of twenty-three volumes,[1] and Sergio Bagú lists over five hundred items in a bibliography which is admittedly incomplete [2]—this from a man who died at the early age of forty-eight. The most important of these works are his *Argentine Sociology, Simulation of Madness and Simulation in the Struggle for Existence* (published together), *Principles of Biological Psychology,* and *Mediocre Man.* All four went through numerous editions.

In general his thought is Darwinian and biological. His interest in the pathology of the individual broadens to include pathology of society as a whole. Even more important, however, was his fundamental reliance on science, and his insistence on the application of science to every aspect of life, even to that of ideals. Like Rodó, his great influence on Latin American youth was due in large measure to his frank appeal to youthful idealism. But unlike Rodó, he felt that science can give us both truth and ideals, and sought a scientific basis and proof of the validity of ideals.

Ingenieros' study of *Simulation in the Struggle for Existence* [3] was one of his most original works. Accepting the general Darwinian theory, he saw two factors, strength and simulation or guile, chiefly responsible for survival and progress. Pretense, evident in every aspect of life from the doctor's bedside manner, and woman's modesty, to claims of racial superiority and nationalism, is a means of defense and survival. Displacement of force by pretense or guile, he said, although leading often to corruption and fraud in society, contributes in the long run to social progress.

His effort to apply scientific principles on a broad social scale is best seen in his *Argentine Sociology,* a work which grew and changed constantly

---

[1] Ingenieros, José. *Obras.* Buenos Aires, L. J. Rosso. 1904-40. 23v.
[2] Bagú, Sergio. *Vida ejemplar de José Ingenieros,* Buenos Aires, Claridad. 1936. 244p.
[3] Published originally in Buenos Aires in 1903 with the *Simulation of Madness.* There are seventeen or eighteen subsequent editions of the two works together and separately.

through at least seven editions.[4] It is a work of the type which has given expression to some of the best social and political thought in Latin America, and which in this case continued the fine Argentine tradition of Echeverría, Alberdi, and Sarmiento. Argentine national development is explained in terms of an economic and biological evolution in which economic principles become a special variety of biological laws. Like Sarmiento, he recognized the close relationship of demographic and political problems, and believed that European immigration determined once and for all the racial composition of Argentina, added greatly to her productive capacity, and would soon end the dominance of landowners and *caudillos* in her political life.

His *Principles of Biological Psychology*[5] is notable for its effort to interpret social phenomena and social behavior psychologically. The treatment of individual and social beliefs as largely irrational has been aptly compared by William Rex Crawford to that of Vilfredo Pareto's *Mind and Society*. In the *Principles of Psychology* he also dealt with what was to be the theme of his later and most famous work, *Mediocre Man*. The idea of "the mediocre man," the enemy of all ideals and progress, is derived from Renan, and had already attracted the interest of Rodó in his *Ariel*. Mediocre man in his beliefs and ambitions is the shadow of the society in which he lives, said Ingenieros. Afraid of being different, he is calculating and tends to measure success in material terms. Simulating belief in old ideals, moral values, and religious faiths, without real inner conviction, he lives a life of hypocrisy.

But progress would be inconceivable without ideals and idealists. Ingenieros believed that ideals have a scientific basis in experience and was interested in their natural history. "The concept of the best is a natural result of evolution itself," he wrote.[6] His ringing denunciations of everything which bespoke ignorance, hypocrisy, reaction, and fear of change made him the spokesman of the spirit of protest, unrest, and rebellion which was gathering force throughout Latin America. His challenging appeal to youth to rebel against mediocrity and give full rein to its natural idealism, made his *Mediocre Man* an even more powerful instrument than Rodó's *Ariel* in shaping the aims and ambitions of a whole generation of Latin American liberal leaders.

Ingenieros was a socialist, but after an early, brief phase of political agitation, conformity to Marxian orthodoxy became less and less characteristic of his thought. Yet he remained a reformer and a man of radical thought. He plunged into the agitation for university reform in 1917-18. The Russian Revolution moved him greatly, and his series of public lec-

[4] Second edition, Madrid, D. Jorro. 1913. 447p. Published originally in Buenos Aires in 1901 as *El determinismo económico en la evolución americana.*
[5] The original title was *Psicología genética.* Buenos Aires, 1911. 364p. The 1919 ed. is included in *Obras completas.* Buenos Aires, L. J. Rosso. [1937] v9. 461p.
[6] *El hombre mediocre.* Santiago de Chile, Ercilla. 1937. p 10.

tures on Russia stirred public opinion greatly. The Russian Revolution had begun a great world movement, he argued, for which the American peoples should be prepared, for it would come to them in some form or other. This interest led naturally to one of his last and greatest studies, a two-volume history of Argentine thought, searching for the historical sense of Argentine development in its revolutionary origins and ideals.

Death found him in 1925 with a number of contemplated works unfinished, including a third volume of his history of Argentine ideas, a study of the genesis of the sensations, a work on metaphysics, and others. He died in the middle of his career. But no other Latin American has set so fine an example of the scientist and teacher who was at the same time an ardent participant in the endless social struggle for the good life. His was, indeed, as Sergio Bagú has said, an exemplary life.

Bagú, Sergio. Vida ejemplar de José Ingenieros, Buenos Aires, Claridad 1936. 244p.

Bermann, Gregorio. José Ingenieros. Buenos Aires, Gleizer. 1926. 208p.

Crawford, W. Rex. A century of Latin-American thought. Cambridge, Harvard University Press. 1944. p 116-42.

Ingenieros, Jose. Obras. Buenos Aires, L. J. Rosso. 1904-40. 23v.

Riaño Juama, Ricardo. Ingenieros y su obra literaria. Habana, Arellano. 1933. 159p.

ANTONIO CASO (1883-1946)

MEXICAN MAESTRO

During the tumultuous years of the Mexican Revolution, the universally respected Antonio Caso stood, sometimes almost alone, calm and unmoved either by the cross currents of divergent revolutionary and counter-revolutionary ideologies which swirled about him, or by the savage forces of civil strife. More than any other contemporary Mexican he attained the preeminent place in Mexican thought formerly held by the great Justo Sierra, though differing radically from him in ideas. Even when he was temporarily out of the good graces of the government and university authorities, the quiet announcement that Antonio Caso would give a course of lectures invariably attracted a large audience of students in Mexico City. José Vasconcelos, whose vitriolic pen has left few of his contemporaries unscathed, made a notable exception in the case of Caso, and joined, during the 1930's, in the chorus of voices of Mexican leaders who demanded his return to the University. Pedro de Alba, Assistant Director of the Pan American Union, calls him the *maestro* of Mexico, and ranks him with Ignacio Ramírez, Ignacio Altamirano, and Justo Sierra in the company of the great mentors of Mexico's intellectual history. His recent death (1946) attracted more attention in the North American press, normally unobservant of Latin American intellectual developments, than that of any other Latin American cultural leader in recent times.

The Mexican artist José Clemente Orozco has painted a portrait of him which reveals in striking fashion the force of his personality. Strong facial features are surmounted by a high forehead and a mass of bushy hair. Heavy eyebrows dominate eyes which flash and burn with the ardent glance which made his lectures an emotional experience never to be forgotten. A determined mouth, with somewhat heavy lips, express the balance and the serenity of his personal life and of his whole philosophy.

Caso was born December 19, 1883 in Mexico City and his education, acquired entirely in the schools of the national capital, was a product of the rich intellectual and cultural development to which the years of peace and prosperity of the Díaz period had given rise in Mexico. He was born into a family which was devoted to education, although its modest means did not permit the study abroad which children of richer families received. His younger brother, Alfonso Caso, became a distinguished archeologist, and has taken an outstanding part in the restoration of some of his country's great archeological monuments.

Antonio soon became marked as a student of independent views who commanded the respect and admiration of his fellow students. While still in the National Preparatory School he began to revolt against the reigning positivist views and to develop a philosophy of life reflecting the new influences emanating from France at the beginning of this century. While still a student he won acclaim for a speech in the newly established Society of Social Studies, a speech in which he defended (against such able opponents as Carlos Pereyra, Vicente Sánchez Gavito, and Ricardo Gómez Robelo) the thesis that aristocratic governments were, on the whole, less defective than democratic ones.

As Caso neared the end of his law course he competed in the examination for the post of professor of universal history in the National Preparatory School. His discourse on the National Convention in the French Revolution clearly won the favor of the audience, and the decision awarding the post to one of the other contenders was hissed by the listeners. The just and kindly Justo Sierra, who presided over the University at this time, relieved somewhat the sting of this disappointment by providing Caso with means to continue his studies. Later he was appointed professor of logic in the National Preparatory School.

He began his teaching career with an eloquent attack on the principles of positivism which had so long ruled Mexican thought and which had been so ably expounded by Justo Sierra. A few years before Caso's death, Alfonso Reyes, the Mexican poet and critic, wrote that it was Caso's eloquent attack which drove positivism from the Mexican scene. While one may well question whether intellectual patterns are changed as quickly and as suddenly as Reyes implies, there is little doubt in the minds of Caso's contemporaries and peers that he exercised a great influence in this direction. José Vasconcelos has called him "the mental liberator, mapping out new paths for the spirit to follow."

For more than thirty years he taught in the National University, and for a time was its rector. He also taught for a time in the Popular or Workers University established during the Revolution. Through his teaching many present-generation Mexicans made their first acquaintance with contemporary European tendencies in thought while at the same time imbibing from the *maestro* principles of intellectual independence. They also acquired confidence in the Mexican, that is to say the American, ability to define human values and orient thought to the American scene without subservience to European patterns.

Caso's revolt against positivism is a part of a much wider revolt against deterministic, positivist and frequently pessimistic thought—a revolt which, in the form of a new humanism, has taken deep root in the Americas. William James represented this tendency in the United States, and many others have followed in his footsteps. In Spanish America there are many representatives: José Rodó and Carlos Vaz Ferreira in Uruguay, Alejandro Deústua in Peru, José Vasconcelos and Samuel Ramos in Mexico. Alejandro Korn, and in some respects even the positivist José Ingenieros, have been its spokesmen in Argentina. Differing much among themselves in many respects, they have agreed upon the importance of defining new human values.

The French philosophers Bergson, Myerson, and, to some extent, Renan, helped to mold Caso's ideas. The ideas of the Russian Nicholas Berdyaev also evoked a special sympathy in his mind. Caso's persistent optimism bespeaks an American spirit. He firmly believed that a new modern age was about to begin, but warned constantly against the possible loss of individualism and liberty as a result of the new tendencies. In his *Filosofía de la cultura y el materialismo histórico (Philosophy of Culture and Historical Materialism)* he warned that the loss of individualism in the new era would threaten the very basis of humanism.[1] The end and purpose of nature, he said, is the person, and culture can only be conceived of as the work of persons. "To be personal is to assume the supreme manifestation of the real."

As has been pointed out, his teaching career began with a general attack on the principles of positivism. Subsequently, in his *Discourses to the Mexican Nation* (1922), he called upon the Mexican people to develop broad and human ideals which could stand contact with life, and the strength to conquer the obstacles which stood in the way of their realization. Rebellion, even for its own sake, he believed, was better than supine acceptance of a reality short of these ideals, and he called upon his countrymen to learn from the writings of Sarmiento a certain "plebeian impulsiveness" and "eternal youthful petulance."

History occupies a large place in Caso's thought. Any complete philosophy he felt, must be based upon history. But history is not a science of the general. Its laws are too difficult to determine to make a science of it, and in some respects it is contradictory even to attempt to define them. This is because history is a normative as well as a cultural study, which deals not only with the facts of being, but with the values embodied and pursued by men. History, therefore, is not a naturalistic science, but "an intuition of that which was."[2] History is understanding and wisdom.

Like Rodó and Renan, Caso believed that an intellectual aristocracy or elite was fundamentally essential to all progress. This concept is closely linked with his ideas of history, for he conceived of progress as coming through the exercise of individual intelligence, and not as a law or principle of history. The aristocratic elite, through its understanding of the past and

---

[1] México, Alba. 1936. p 154-9. "Renan y Berdiaeff."
[2] Quoted from *Problemas filosóficos* in W. Rex Crawford's *A Century of Latin-American Thought.* Cambridge, Harvard University Press. 1944. p282.

through its intelligence, forms the link between tradition and progress. Yet in spite of his emphasis upon personalism, individualism, and the role of an intellectual elite, Caso's philosophy was not in any sense unsocial. This appears clearly in his *Genetic and Systematic Sociology*. In fact, contradictory as it might seem on the surface, the irreducible social element for him was not the individual but the group. It was only in and through the culture in which he lived that the individual achieved the full development of his personality, and action in the social scene was the natural corollary and result of historical and social understanding. Hence at the age of twenty-five Caso helped to found the Ateneo de Juventud, in which he initiated a great national cultural crusade with José Vasconcelos, Pedro Henríquez Ureña, González Martínez, and Alfonso Reyes.

Many of the leaders of the Mexican Revolution were his fellow students, colleagues in the University, or fellow members in the Ateneo de Juventud, the intellectual center from which emanated so much of the ideology of the Revolution during its earlier phases. Yet he himself took no active part in the movement. During the revolutionary years he succeeded, even though frequently against great pressure, in keeping himself clear of political commitments, quietly continuing to teach the oncoming generation of Mexican youth the broadly humanistic principles and outlook which guided his thought.

Caso's most inspiring book was his *Discourses to the Mexican Nation*, published in 1922. It is a strong and forceful appeal to all thinking Mexicans to develop ideals and the will to pursue them in eliminating the defects and weaknesses of the national political life and renovating the national culture. He called for a program of education which would lose its fear of new ideas and center on the development of students' personalities. "The world is still unfinished," he wrote, and the perfection of its defects was the best of motives to human action. It alone gave meaning to human life. He called upon all Mexicans to develop their hidden potentialities for good, not to accept the low aim of pleasure, but rather the pleasure of courageous pursuit of social aims. "The first vice is laziness and the first virtue enthusiasm."

Like many Latin American intellectuals Caso felt a stirring of sympathy for German National Socialism because of its apparent appeal for spiritual regeneration. The way had been prefaced by the growing Latin American interest in German social thought. This appears in his *New Discourses to the Mexican Nation* in 1934, in which he hailed with enthusiasm the fact that the same tendencies seemed to be represented in National Socialism and in the new policies of the Roosevelt administration. But disillusionment soon followed as the anti-liberal aspects of totalitarianism became more clearly evident. In his 1941 volume, *The Human Personality and the Totalitarian State*, he redefined his political position in a more mature defense of democracy with all its defects. Democracy and liberty, precious as they are, are but a means to an end, the cultural and spiritual development of man. Tyranny is that which crushes the spirit of man and puts shackles on his free thinking. But democracies need to guard against the chaos of complete individualism which may in the end be just as destructive. The danger of totalitarianism lay in its deification of the State. If the State declares itself above all law then the individual, too, can declare himself above all principles. On the whole, he concludes, while modern democracies fall far short of achieving their proper aims, their failure is still far from that of totalitarianism, and the new age which is emerging must achieve its aims through democratic instrumentalities.

The same theme runs through much of Caso's subsequent writing. In *Man's Danger* (1942) he returned to the threat to human personality which totalitarianism presented, and to what is the principal key to all his thought, the role of human personality in the creation of values of all kinds. In the striking cross fertilization of ideas and the intellectual renaissance which the Spanish Civil War and the war years brought to Mexico, Caso received enhanced prestige and even greater national recognition as new books streamed from his pen. After he had been reinstated in the University, he was made Honorary Director of the Faculty of Philosophy and Letters. His sudden death, early in March 1946, cut short the life of one of Mexico's greatest intellectual figures, and one of the great minds of contemporary America.

José Vasconelos paid tribute to Caso in a funeral oration:

Your written work is clear, abundant and representative of the Mexican [spirit]. . . . But greater than it is your career as *maestro.*

The Americas. 3:20-30. July 1946. A Mexican personalist. Kurt F. Reinhardt.

Books Abroad. 20 no 3:238-42. 1946. Antonio Caso, Mexican philosopher. Kurt F. Reinhardt.

Bulletin of the Pan American Union. 80:425-8. August 1946. Antonio Caso, el maestro, in memoriam. Pedro de Alba.

Crawford, W. Rex. A century of Latin-American thought. Cambridge, Harvard University Press. 1944. p276-92 and *passim.*

Latin American Thought. Vol. I, no. 3. April 1946. John H. Hershey, ed.

Letras de México. January 15, 1941. Apuntes sobre la filosofía en México. A. Menéndez Samará.

New York Times. p21. March 8, 1946. Antonio Caso, Mexican philosopher, 1883-1946.

Philosophy and Phenomenological Research. 3:127-134. December 1943. Tendencias contemporáneas en el pensamiento hispano-americana. Francisco Romero.

Poviña, Alfredo. Historia de la sociología latino-américana. México, Fondo de Cultura Económica. 1941. p 126-29.

Publicaciones de la Universidad de Santo Domingo. 42:17-38. 1946. Antonio Caso, un filósofo de América. Joaquín E. Salazar.

Revista mexicana de sociología. 8:15-36. January-April 1946. Antonio Caso y su obra. Eduardo García Máynez.

Time. 47:86. March 18, 1946.

Todo. p 15. March 21, 1946. Antonio Caso. Nemesio García Naranjo.

Unity. p 30-31. April 1943. Antonio Caso: Mexican personalist. John H. Hershey.

INDEX